FRANCIS FRITH'S
LINCOLN - A HISTORY AND CELEBRATION

THE FRANCIS FRITH COLLECTION

www.francisfrith.com

LINCOLN
A HISTORY & CELEBRATION

CRAIG SPENCE

THE FRANCIS FRITH COLLECTION

www.francisfrith.com

First published in the United Kingdom in 2004
by The Francis Frith Collection®

Hardback edition 2004 ISBN 1-90493-835-3
Paperback edition 2012 ISBN 978-1-84589-641-6

Text and Design copyright © The Francis Frith Collection®
Photographs copyright © The Francis Frith Collection®
except where indicated

The Frith® photographs and the Frith® logo are reproduced under licence from Heritage Photographic Resources Ltd, the owners of the Frith® archive and trademarks
'The Francis Frith Collection', 'Francis Frith' and 'Frith' are registered trademarks of Heritage Photographic Resources Ltd.

All rights reserved. No photograph in this publication may be sold to a third party other than in the original form of this publication, or framed for sale to a third party. No parts of this publication may be reproduced, stored in a retrieval system, or transmitted, in any form, or by any means, electronic, mechanical, photocopying, recording or otherwise, without the prior permission of the publishers and copyright holder.

British Library Cataloguing in Publication Data

Lincoln - A History & Celebration
Craig Spence

The Francis Frith Collection®
Oakley Business Park, Wylye Road,
Dinton, Wiltshire SP3 5EU
Tel: +44 (0) 1722 716 376
Email: info@francisfrith.co.uk
www.francisfrith.com

Printed and bound in Great Britain
Contains material sourced from responsibly managed forests

Front Cover: **LINCOLN, HIGH STREET c1950** L49028t

Additional modern photographs by Craig Spence.

Domesday extract used in timeline by kind permission of
Alecto Historical Editions, www.domesdaybook.org
Aerial photographs reproduced under licence from
Simmons Aerofilms Limited.
Historical Ordnance Survey maps reproduced under licence from
Homecheck.co.uk

Every attempt has been made to contact copyright holders of
illustrative material. We will be happy to give full acknowledgement in future editions for any items not credited. Any information should be directed to The Francis Frith Collection.

*The colour-tinting in this book is for illustrative purposes only,
and is not intended to be historically accurate*

AS WITH ANY HISTORICAL DATABASE, THE FRANCIS FRITH ARCHIVE IS CONSTANTLY BEING CORRECTED AND IMPROVED, AND THE PUBLISHERS WOULD WELCOME INFORMATION ON OMISSIONS OR INACCURACIES

CONTENTS

6	Timeline
8	Chapter 1 : Roman, Anglo-Saxon and Viking Lincoln
26	Chapter 2 : Medieval and Later Lincoln
56	Chapter 3 : Victorian Lincoln
78	Chapter 4 : 20th Century Lincoln
106	Chapter 5 : Lincoln Today
117	Acknowledgements and Bibliography
119	Free Mounted Print Offer

LINCOLN
A History & Celebration

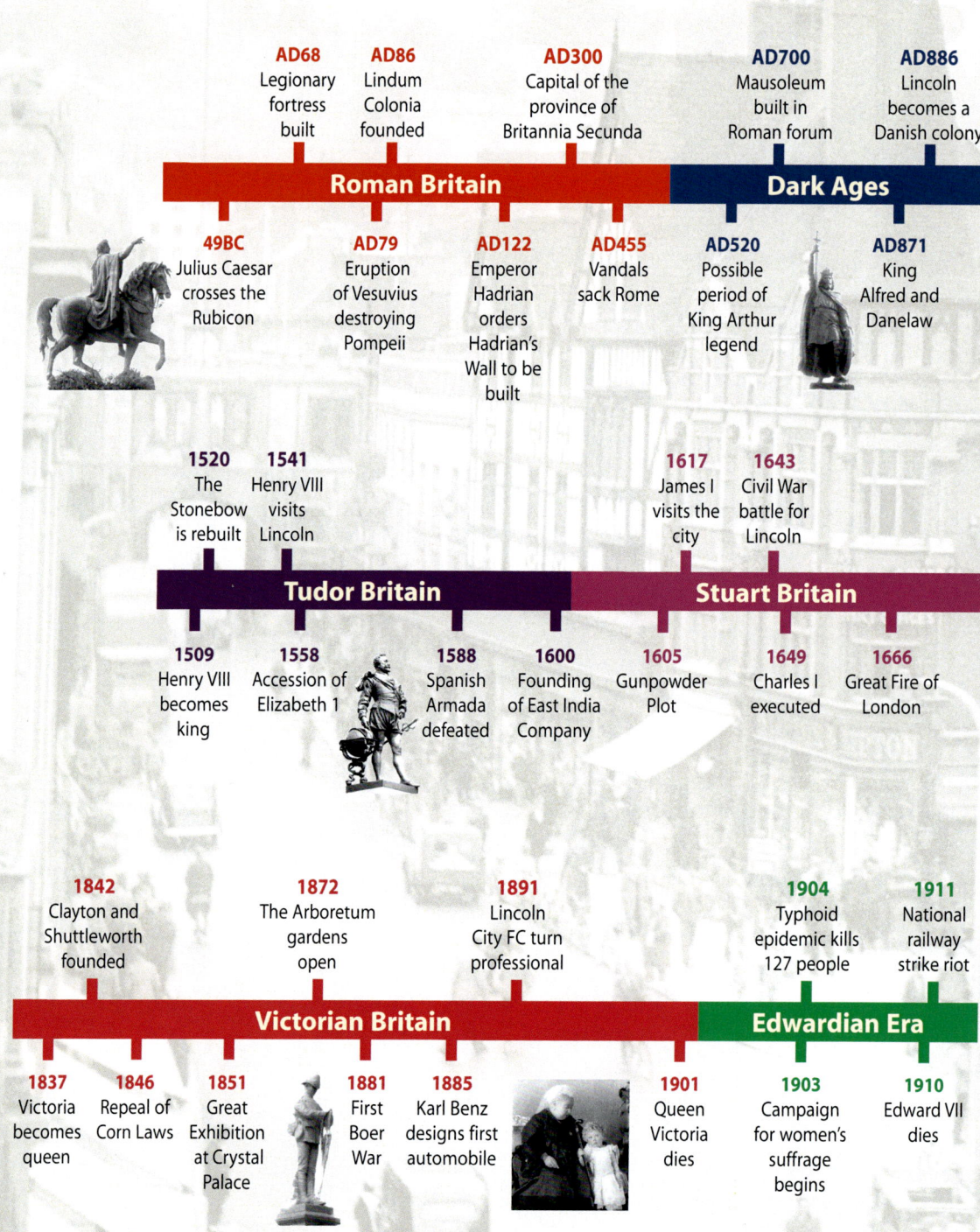

Roman Britain

- **AD68** Legionary fortress built
- **AD86** Lindum Colonia founded
- **AD300** Capital of the province of Britannia Secunda
- **49BC** Julius Caesar crosses the Rubicon
- **AD79** Eruption of Vesuvius destroying Pompeii
- **AD122** Emperor Hadrian orders Hadrian's Wall to be built
- **AD455** Vandals sack Rome

Dark Ages

- **AD700** Mausoleum built in Roman forum
- **AD886** Lincoln becomes a Danish colony
- **AD520** Possible period of King Arthur legend
- **AD871** King Alfred and Danelaw

Tudor Britain

- **1520** The Stonebow is rebuilt
- **1541** Henry VIII visits Lincoln
- **1509** Henry VIII becomes king
- **1558** Accession of Elizabeth 1
- **1588** Spanish Armada defeated
- **1600** Founding of East India Company

Stuart Britain

- **1617** James I visits the city
- **1643** Civil War battle for Lincoln
- **1605** Gunpowder Plot
- **1649** Charles I executed
- **1666** Great Fire of London

Victorian Britain

- **1842** Clayton and Shuttleworth founded
- **1872** The Arboretum gardens open
- **1891** Lincoln City FC turn professional
- **1837** Victoria becomes queen
- **1846** Repeal of Corn Laws
- **1851** Great Exhibition at Crystal Palace
- **1881** First Boer War
- **1885** Karl Benz designs first automobile

Edwardian Era

- **1904** Typhoid epidemic kills 127 people
- **1911** National railway strike riot
- **1901** Queen Victoria dies
- **1903** Campaign for women's suffrage begins
- **1910** Edward VII dies

HISTORICAL TIMELINE FOR LINCOLN

Middle Ages / Late Medieval

- **1068** Lincoln Castle founded
- **1092** First cathedral consecrated
- **1185** Earthquake destroys the cathedral
- **1217** 'Battle of Lincoln Fair'
- **1326** Lincoln becomes a staple town
- **1450** Population of city reaches low of 1,750

- **1066** Battle of Hastings. Norman rule begins
- **1086** Domesday Book
- **1170** Murder of Thomas à Becket at Canterbury cathedral
- **1215** Magna Carta
- **1306** Robert the Bruce declares himself King of Scotland
- **1348** Black Death kills 25 million in Europe
- **1415** Battle of Agincourt
- **1485** Battle of Bosworth Field marks end of Plantaganet dynasty

Georgian Era

- **1736** Butter Market constructed
- **1745** Bailgate Assembly Rooms built
- **1777** City Hospital founded
- **1815** George Boole born in Silver Street
- **1820** The Lawn lunatic asylum opens

- **1739** John Wesley founds Methodist church
- **1762** Mozart performs at the age of 6
- **1789** French Revolution
- **1815** Battle of Waterloo
- **1825** Stockton to Darlington Railway

20th Century Britain

- **1916** William Foster Ltd build world's first tank
- **1927** Usher Gallery opens
- **1958** Pelham Bridge opened by the Queen
- **1964** Last Lincoln Races meeting
- **1982** First Christmas Market
- **1996** University of Lincoln founded

- **1914** First World War begins
- **1926** John Logie Baird obtains first television picture
- **1939** Outbreak of Second World War
- **1956** Suez Crisis
- **1966** England win World Cup
- **1969** First man on the Moon
- **1982** Falklands Conflict

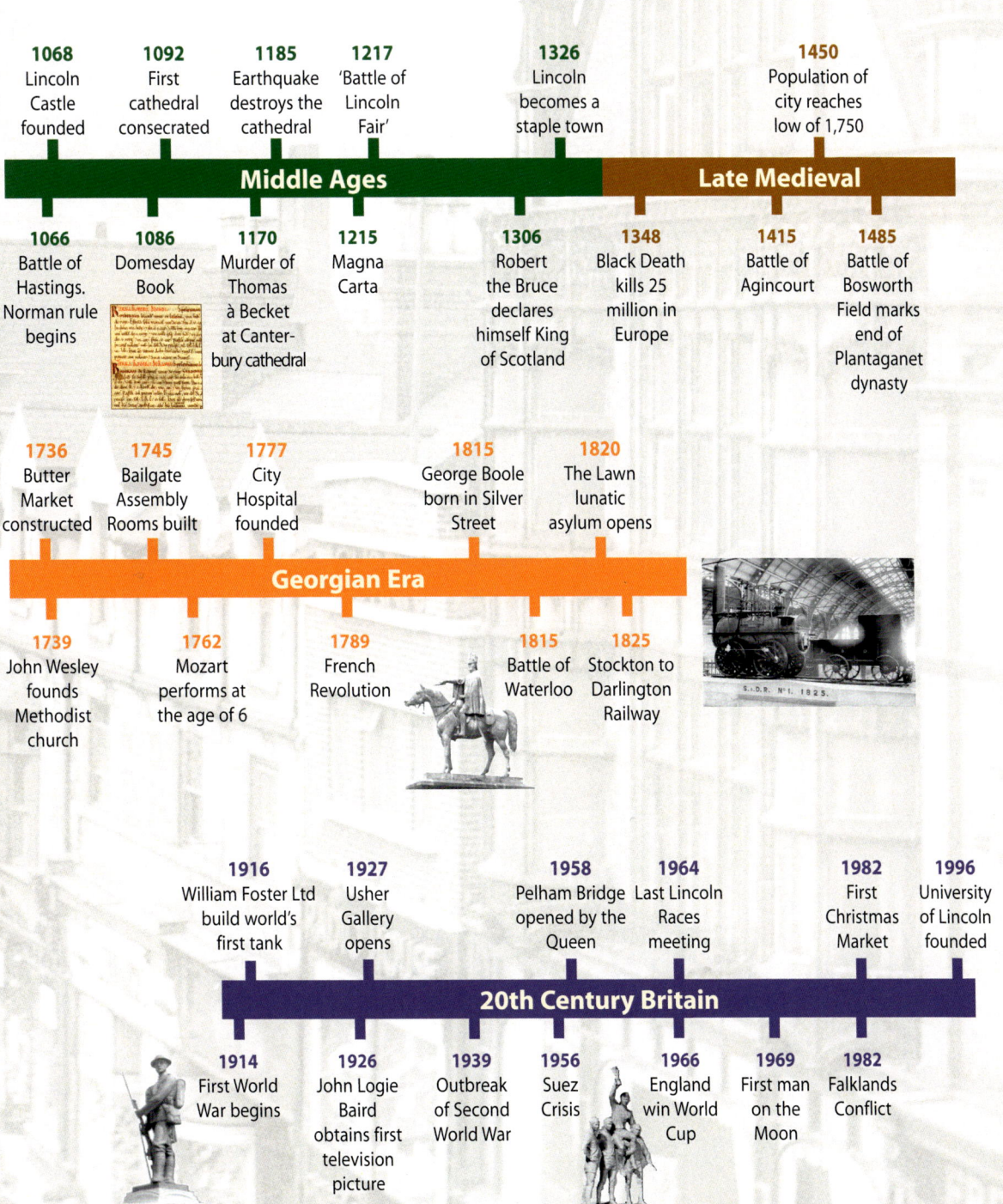

CHAPTER ONE

ROMAN, ANGLO-SAXON AND VIKING LINCOLN

A HISTORY & CELEBRATION

WHEN THE Roman soldiers of the IX legion 'Hispana' marched toward the River Witham, as it flowed slowly through the gap in the limestone ridge escarpment now known as the Lincoln Edge, they saw little apart from trees and a few breaths of wispy smoke rising above a collection of Iron Age huts grouped by the side of a shallow lake. Crossing the river and making the steep sixty-five metre climb out of the valley, they were clearly struck by the defensive possibilities of the hilltop location that overlooked the vast expanse of land running away westward toward the river Trent. As their officers and surveyors conferred, it soon became clear this would be the place to build a great legionary fortress protecting the meeting point of the Roman roads of Ermine Street and the earlier Fosse Way.

The exact date of this founding event is unknown, but the legions of the Emperor Claudius had arrived on the south coast of Britain in AD 43, making their way slowly northward. It is likely that substantial numbers of troops arrived in the Lincoln area a little over ten years later. The construction of the legionary fortress, capable of housing some 5,000 men, was certainly complete by AD 68. Evidence for the earlier, pre-fortress, period is less clear-cut. To the south of the present city, in the area of Monson Street close to the High Street, a number of military gravestones were found in the 19th century. This suggests that the Romans may have set up a temporary encampment in that area before moving to the hilltop position. But what of the people who already occupied the site, the

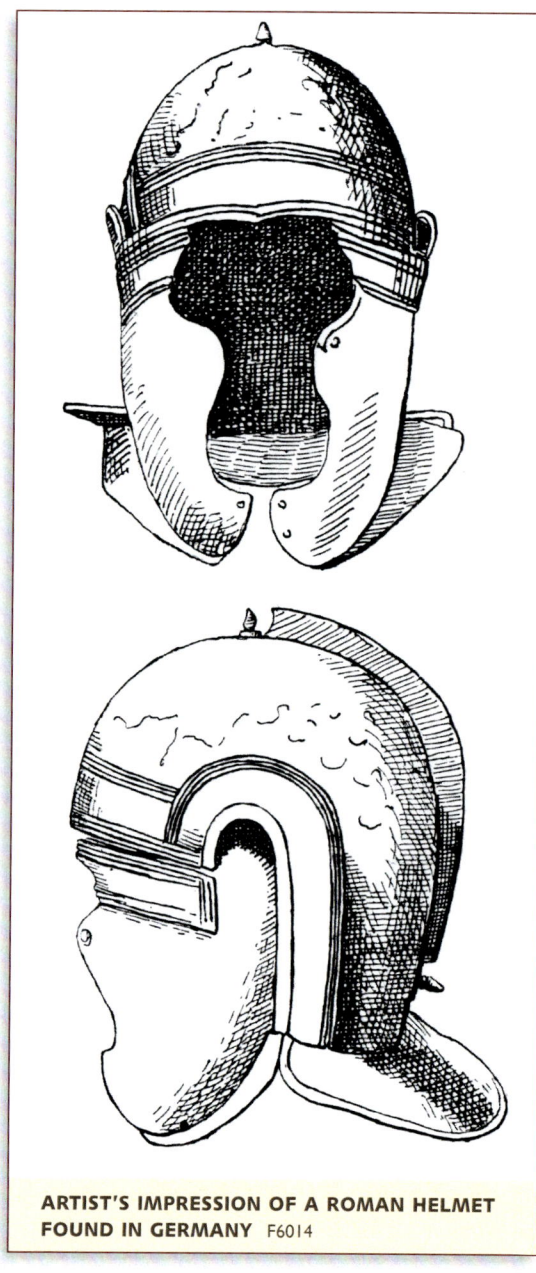

ARTIST'S IMPRESSION OF A ROMAN HELMET FOUND IN GERMANY F6014

Corieltauvi? They seem to have occupied a small settlement on the shore of the lake formed by the confluence of the rivers Till and Witham—a lake that still dominates the city in the form of Brayford Pool.

ROMAN, ANGLO-SAXON AND VIKING LINCOLN

OLD ROMAN GATE 1890 25660

The famous Newport Arch dates from the second century AD. The building on the left has since been demolished, allowing the pavement to be moved outside of the archway.

The founding of Lincoln as we now know it can be best linked with the construction of the great legionary fortress, one of only nine in Britain. In its earliest form the fort comprised turf ramparts, fronted by a wall of timber planking, surrounded by an extensive ditch. The fort enclosed an area some 440 x 360 metres, and the position of its walls and gateways can still be discerned in the arrangement of streets in the uphill area of the city. The principal gateway to the fort lay to the east on Eastgate, where the remains of a timber structure with a double carriageway were discovered in 1966. Elements of this structure, the 'porta praetoria', can still be seen displayed some 3 or 4 metres below street level outside the Lincoln Hotel.

The streets inside the fortress were lined with barrack blocks and other buildings. In the centre of the fortress lay the 'principia', the headquarters building. This took the form of a hall and courtyard complex, in the north-east corner of which a well was sunk some 15 metres into the underlying deposits. The wellhead was rebuilt in the second century AD, and can now be seen at the junction of Bailgate and Westgate.

A History & Celebration

Despite all this activity the formal military presence was short-lived. The IX legion advanced northward in AD 71, to be replaced by the II legion 'Adiutrix' who in turn departed in AD 78. Instead of ordering further troops into the area the Roman administration, with the direct approval of the emperor, chose to designate the settlement as a 'colonia', a town of great importance dedicated to retired soldiers. This turned a military settlement into a strongly Romanised civilian one, dominated as it was by the presence of many hundreds of ex-soldiers. It is likely that this change occurred soon after AD 86.

The new settlement came to be known as Lindum Colonia, the Celtic word for a pool or lake being 'Lind'. But it is from this Roman renaming that we arrive at today's name for the city, Lincoln. One of the first phases of activity in building the new city was the creation of the streets. Several of the surviving fort streets, in what was to become known as the upper city, were provided with drains or sewers and then resurfaced. These streets followed a grid pattern, which then extended outside the fort walls to the south on either side of Ermine Street (now the High Street) as far as the river.

At the beginning of the second century AD work started on rebuilding the walls of the upper city. The line of the new walls, built of local limestone, followed that of the earlier fort. The gates were also rebuilt in stone. One such gate still stands as a unique survival from this period, the Newport Arch, which is located at the northern end of Bailgate. What makes it unique, at least in Britain, is its continued use for road traffic; though this was nearly its undoing in 1964 when an over-height lorry attempted to pass beneath it, causing considerable damage.

A council made up of 100 councillors, known as 'decurions', ran the new city. One such Lincoln decurion was Aurelius Senecio, who in the 3rd century had the sad task of erecting a tombstone for his wife Volusia Faustina, who had died at the relatively young age of 26. Such a large town council would of course require a suitable town hall. The Roman equivalent of such a building was the forum and basilica complex. It is clear that Lincoln had a series of two such complexes, the first of which was constructed in the early 2nd century and which was replaced sometime in the early 3rd century.

Fact File

Ermine Street

If you had asked a Roman inhabitant of Lincoln the way to Ermine Street they would not have known what you were talking about! The name 'Ermine' actually dates from the Saxon period, and is thought to have been associated with a group of people known as the Earningas who lived in a part of Cambridgeshire through which the road passed.

ROMAN, ANGLO-SAXON AND VIKING LINCOLN

STEEP HILL c1955 L49063

The upper part of Steep Hill exactly overlies the line of the Roman road known as Ermine Street.

LINCOLN
A HISTORY & CELEBRATION

THE 'MINT WALL', A PART OF THE ROMAN BASILICA 2004
ZZZ01599 (Zoe Tomlinson)

This later and larger structure lay in the centre of the upper city. It comprised a large basilica situated to the north of an open courtyard known as the forum, which was in turn surrounded on three sides by ranges of masonry buildings with internal porticos. It is likely that the complex was completed with the addition of a major temple precinct to the south of the forum.

The basilica was a monumental structure standing over 9 metres high and occupying an area about 13 x 70 metres. On the east the entire complex fronted onto the main north-south street now represented by Bailgate. That frontage consisted of a covered way supported on 19 stone columns. The colonnade first came to light during building works in 1878; today the position of the columns has been marked with stone setts in the road surface of Bailgate.

The forum was in part an open public space adorned with statues, but there were also associated buildings that have been excavated. They were found to include rooms used as shops or workshops and a room that contained the rebuilt wellhead. The precinct further south is likely to have been the location for the temple of the imperial cult. One of the priests of the cult in Lincoln was Marcus Aurelius Lunaris, a successful wine merchant. It is likely that other temples and public buildings were also constructed within the walled upper city, which was also the site for the main public bathhouse.

The baths complex was located in the north-east corner of the upper city and consisted of a series of heated and unheated rooms, plunge-baths and a gymnasium area. Bathhouses required a substantial supply of water if they were to function properly; consequently extra water was brought to Lincoln from outside the city. Lincoln's aqueduct was little more than a ceramic pipe, 15 cm in diameter, encased in hydraulic concrete but it served its purpose. Possibly drawing water from the Roaring Meg springhead to the north-east of the city, or more likely from the distant Wolds, the aqueduct

ROMAN, ANGLO-SAXON AND VIKING LINCOLN

> ## Fact File
>
> ### The Mint Wall
>
> *Lincoln boasts a unique survival from Roman Britain, the so-called Mint Wall, which can be seen in West Bight immediately behind the Castle Hotel. This massive piece of masonry is part of the north wall of the basilica and still stands over 7 metres high and 23 metres in length. It is considered to be the largest non-defensive masonry structure to survive from the Roman period in Britain.*

south along either side of Ermine Street, now the High Street. Dividing the two 'cities' was the upper city's south wall, pierced in its centre by the upper south gate.

From this point the street drops sharply down the hillside. The Romans overcame the severe incline by paving the street with large stone steps. On either side of these, great retaining walls supported terraces, on which were constructed further public buildings, including perhaps a theatre. The steps would have hindered the passage of wheeled vehicles so a zig-zag diversion was constructed to the east. This diversion still exists in part in the form of Well Lane and Danesgate, and continues to provide a marginally less strenuous ascent for those amongst us who want to bypass the steepest part of Steep Hill!

was carried over a small valley on a series of regular stone-built piers before being buried underground on its approach to the city. At least one branch of the aqueduct arrived at the north wall just to the east of the Newport Arch and fed a large masonry tank capable of holding around 12,000 litres of water. The position and partial remains of this water tank can still be seen in a garden to the north of East Bight.

While the core of the early civilian settlement was located within the boundary of the earlier fortress, further areas of occupation spilled down the hillside and extended

WELL LANE 2004 L4970lk (Craig Spence)

Well Lane follows the line of the Roman road that diverted around the steps of Ermine Street and provided a gentler climb up the hillside for wheeled vehicles.

15

LINCOLN
A HISTORY & CELEBRATION

THE UPPER SOUTH GATE

Until recently the upper south gate was thought to have consisted of a single carriageway, with possible pedestrian portals on either side, similar in design to the Newport Arch. Yet antiquarian drawings from the 18th century seemed to suggest that this was not the case, and that the structure actually had two archways.

ENGRAVING OF THE REMAINS OF THE ROMAN UPPER SOUTH GATE LOOKING NORTH 1788
ZZZ01589 (Lincolnshire County Council, Local Studies Collection)

REMAINS OF THE WESTERN SIDE OF THE ROMAN UPPER SOUTH GATE ON STEEP HILL 2004 L49702k (Craig Spence)

The matter was finally resolved in 2001, when refurbishment of 44 Steep Hill revealed the side wall of the 'unknown' eastern carriageway, and also stones of the 'spina' or dividing wall between the two carriageways. The earlier remnants of the gate had been removed or concealed during 19th century rebuilding work. These new discoveries can now be seen within the premises of the shop that occupies the building. On the opposite side of Steep Hill a small vertical strip of honey-coloured masonry represents the surviving part of the side wall of the western carriageway.

ROMAN, ANGLO-SAXON AND VIKING LINCOLN

Merchants, traders and artisans crowded into the lower city. Many of these individuals were very wealthy, as indicated by the mosaic floors and other decorative features discovered during excavations on either side of the High Street. Such opulent development of masonry buildings probably took place from the mid 2nd century onwards. The frontages of Roman Ermine Street as it passed through the lower city were lined with substantial public buildings, including a fountain built of massive limestone blocks, the remains of which were discovered beneath 291–292 High Street.

Initially the buildings of the lower city spread across the hillside and waterside to both the east and west, but all broadly respected a street grid that drew its orientation from that of the upper city. In the late 2nd or early 3rd century a decision was taken, probably in response to some imminent danger, to enclose the lower city behind substantial defensive walls. Two north-south walls were constructed, originating from the southern corners of the upper city's defences. They ran downhill to the River Witham. An east-west wall along the waterside completed the

The current Stonebow is on the site of the Roman south gate, and perhaps represents the general form of that earlier structure, though the building we see today dates from the 16th century.

circuit. During the 4th century the existing upper city walls were strengthened and the outer ditch greatly widened. Today the ditch can best be viewed from East Bight by looking north across the gardens of houses fronting Church Lane.

The walls of the lower city were clearly pierced in several places by gates, including the points where the wall crosses the line of modern day West Parade and Monks Road. The most important gate must have been that across Ermine Street to the south. This may in fact represent the site of an earlier triumphal arch that greeted visitors to the city even before the walls were built. In the southern length of the western wall a new gateway was inserted some time in the later 4th century. This reused monumental stonework possibly taken from the adjacent cemetery. The base of this gateway and parts of the wall can be seen today in the car park immediately north of City Hall. Another much smaller gate was inserted into the southern wall some 100 metres east of Ermine Street during the late Roman period. This was a postern gate constructed to control, and tax, those moving between the walled city and the wharfs of the waterside. Found during excavations in 1974, the postern gate has been preserved in a basement area beneath the modern Stonebow Centre.

Beyond the city to the south lay a neighbourhood of traders and artisans occupying strip buildings whose narrow ends faced onto Ermine Street, or, further south, the Fosse Way. These buildings were some 8 metres wide and up to 30 metres long, and included shop, workshop and living space within their length. There is evidence for the existence of various trades, including metalworking, shoemaking, and the use of ovens for food or industrial production. The attraction for residents of this thriving manufacturing suburb must have been the roads and their travellers, but also the nearby river and its potential for transport.

REMAINS OF THE ROMAN LOWER CITY WEST GATE 2004 L49703k (Craig Spence)

ROMAN, ANGLO-SAXON AND VIKING LINCOLN

EASTGATE c1955 L49108

Eastgate follows the line of the Roman road that ran along the crest of the river valley toward the Greetwell Villa, perhaps the residence of the 3rd century provincial governor.

The Fosse Way joined Ermine Street at a point some 700 metres to the south of the southern gate, near to the junction of the modern-day High Street and King Street. Houses lined both sides of the roads for another 200 metres south of the road junction. Beyond that point the roads passed through a collection of tombs and monuments in an area dedicated to burials, and thus beyond the formal limits of the Roman settlement. The wheel-rutted surface of the Fosse Way can still be seen under a glass floor inserted into a room within the magnificent St Mary's Guildhall, which is itself of medieval date.

At the end of the 3rd century Roman Britain was reorganised into four lesser provinces, and Lincoln was elevated to the status of the provincial capital of one of these, 'Britannia Secunda'. It is possible that the magnificent buildings discovered about a mile east of the city during the 1880s, known as the Greetwell Villa, made up the extramural residence of the new provincial governor. It was certainly a vast and richly decorated structure with painted wall plaster and mosaic floors of the very highest quality. Unfortunately the structure was completely destroyed by late 19th century quarrying activity.

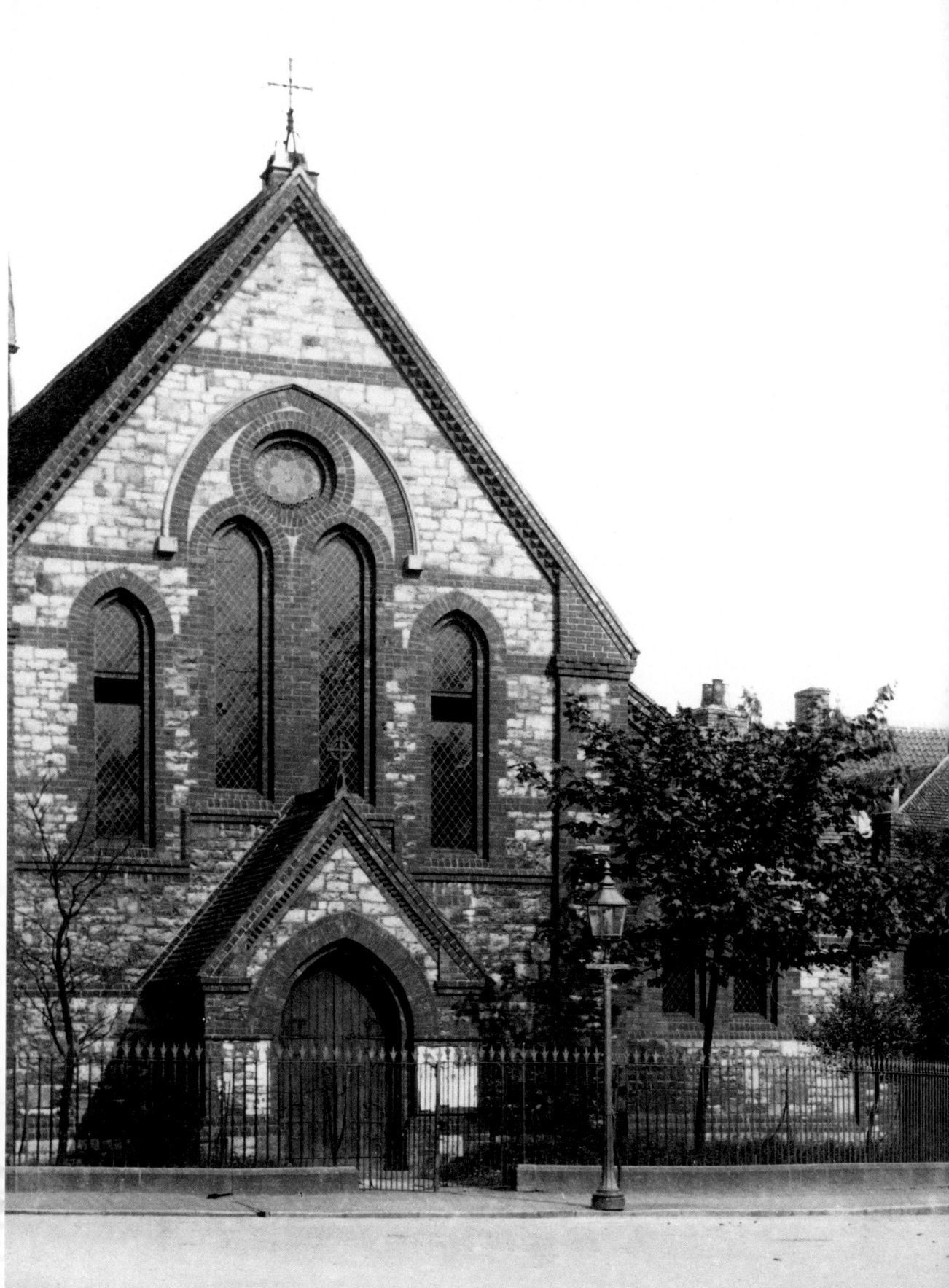

ST PAUL'S CHURCH AND CATHEDRAL 1890 25655

LINCOLN
A HISTORY & CELEBRATION

The presence of the Greetwell Villa together with other economic indicators suggests that Lincoln in the later 3rd century was still a reasonably prosperous and well-organised place. The city had nurtured an early Christian community and in 314 Lincoln sent its bishop, Adelphius, to the first Christian Council at Arles. It is the combined presence of a provincial administration and religious community that help to explain the probable survival of urban life beyond the end of Roman rule. Roman Britain officially came to an end in the year 410, though of course the Romans did not 'go home' as by that date most of the inhabitants of Britain's cities were indigenous people who simply led a Roman life-style. In this Lincoln was no different and there is good evidence for continued activity within the city well into the 5th century. The population of the city was however much reduced, and the people lived in inferior conditions.

Perhaps the most likely focus for true continuity of settlement is to be found in the upper city. Here at some time in the 4th or 5th century a small church was constructed within the area of the forum. This building was replaced, probably during the 5th century but possibly as late as the 7th, by a new church with an apsidal east end and evidence for a chancel screen. The ground plan of this church can now be seen marked in the open space at the junction of Westgate and Bailgate, the site previously occupied by St Paul in the Bail, which was demolished in 1971. These early churches are very important discoveries as there are only a handful of possible Romano-British churches known in the country.

The central positioning of this church within the prestigious forum of a provincial capital reflects a very high level of ecclesiastical authority. The most famous bishop present in Lincoln during the early 7th century was Paulinus. Later canonised, St Paulinus undertook the conversion of the local population to Christianity and was known to have built a cathedral church in Lincoln by 630. We cannot say for sure that this was the site of that structure but it is an idea worthy of some serious consideration.

Taking a wider view, and going back a little in time, we find that by the beginning of the 6th century Roman Lincoln had ceased to function as a city, certainly as an economic centre. It is possible that an ecclesiastical, or aristocratic, centre still operated within the walls of the upper

ARTIST'S IMPRESSION OF SAXON HOUSES F6015

ROMAN, ANGLO-SAXON AND VIKING LINCOLN

> ## Fact File
>
> ### Gates and Streets
>
> *The term 'gate' in street names such as Danesgate or Saltergate does not refer to an entrance but has its origin in the Danish word 'gata', which simply meant street. In the same vein the name Stonebow finds its roots in the Danish phrase 'steinn boga' meaning a stone archway. From this we know that the Roman south gate was still standing in the ninth century.*

city; nonetheless this would be against a backdrop of widespread abandonment, decay and ruination. During the 5th and 6th centuries Saxon settlers from northern Europe established the kingdom of Lindsey across that part of the county north of the Witham, but although Lincoln clearly contributed its name to the new kingdom there is no evidence that the city formed its capital. Lindsey was never of great power and was by turns dominated by the kingdoms of Northumbria and Mercia, thus relegating it to the status of a sub-kingdom or province.

If there was activity within Lincoln during this early Saxon period its precise location remains unclear. Finds of pottery of this date have been recovered from both the upper and lower city but in small numbers, relatively larger numbers of sherds have been recovered from the area just outside the upper west gate. Could this be the site of an early Saxon settlement or meeting place?

Stronger evidence exists to support the idea of an ecclesiastical centre within the upper city. Sometime during or soon after the 7th century a large square mausoleum or chapel was constructed over the site of the earlier church at St Paul in the Bail. At its centre lay a stone-lined grave from which, at some time in the past, the burial had been removed. The removal, or translation, of saint's remains occurred frequently during this period, and that may be the explanation here. But hidden or overlooked within the stone lining was a single artefact, a magnificent enamelled hanging bowl of Anglo-Saxon date. The bowl can now be seen in the treasury of Lincoln Cathedral.

Later in the Saxon period the lower city, particularly the south-east corner, began to see signs of renewed activity. While Ermine Street continued in use throughout the period it is clear that most of the earlier Roman street grid was lost. Among the new streets carved out of this ruinous landscape were Silver Street, a diagonal cut-through between the Stonebow and the gateway in the eastern wall, and Clasketgate, which ran west towards the High Street.

During the 9th century succeeding Viking armies over-ran the east midlands. In 886 King Alfred was forced to surrender Lincoln and so began the city's period as a Viking or Danish colony. The new settlers occupied the city in large numbers and made concerted efforts to turn the rubble-strewn

A HISTORY & CELEBRATION

SILVER STREET c1950 L49011

environment into a thriving commercial city and port. They were surprisingly successful. Further new roads were laid out, including Hungate, Flaxengate, Danesgate and Saltergate, street names that remain with us today.

The Danish city was a hive of activity, craft-workers, traders and merchants jostled for position among the timber and thatched houses that lined the new streets. The waterfront was key to the development of the city and efforts to reclaim the waterside areas were begun at

ROMAN, ANGLO-SAXON AND VIKING LINCOLN

Lincoln between the mid 10th and 11th centuries. Only London had more. As the city grew in size the old Roman suburb south of the Witham was reborn, becoming known as Wigford. Suburbs to the east and west of the lower city walls also developed at this time.

Later in the period the pagan Danish began to adhere to the Christian religion. This led to the foundation of a number of new churches within the city and suburbs probably from the year 1014 onwards. Of most importance amongst the surviving church buildings are St Mary-le-Wigford and St Peter at Gowts, both on the lower High Street. Both have fine square towers that date from the 11th century. In the wall of the tower of St Mary-le-Wigford is a Roman gravestone that was reused as a dedicatory tablet by the founder, a man named Eirtig. He endowed the church 'to the glory of Christ and St Mary'. A thousand years later Eirtig's tablet still looks down on the people of Lincoln as they hurry back and forth along the modern High Street.

ROMAN GRAVESTONE RE-USED AS A SAXON DEDICATORY TABLET IN THE TOWER OF ST MARY-LE-WIGFORD CHURCH 2004 ZZZ01600 (Zoe Tomlinson)

this time. Merchants imported both everyday and exotic objects and goods from elsewhere in Britain, across Europe and even further afield. The increased economic status was reflected in the number of city mints that were set up to produce coin. Some ninety-five moneyers were working in

25

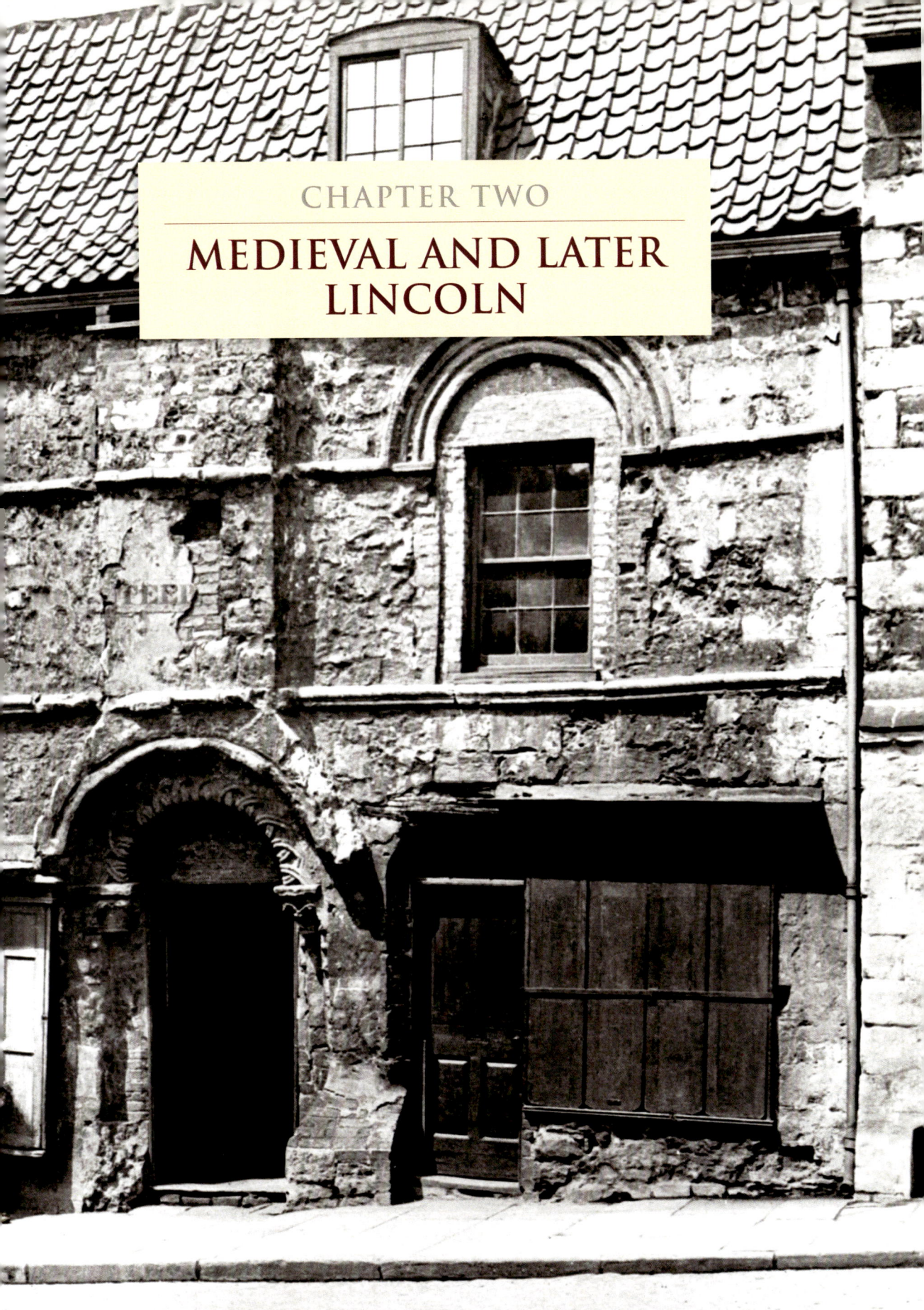

CHAPTER TWO

MEDIEVAL AND LATER LINCOLN

A HISTORY & CELEBRATION

WHEN THE conquering army of William Duke of Normandy arrived in Lincoln following the invasion of 1066 they found a busy and prosperous city of around some 8,000 people. Its wealth and size made Lincoln the third greatest city in the land, only outranked marginally by York and rather more decidedly by London. The people of the city were largely Anglo-Danish in origin and were able to maintain their cultural identity in the face of the Norman advance for a number of years.

Amongst the leading citizens of Lincoln were the Twelve Lawmen who governed the city through various courts and meetings, or moots. Among this group were men with names such as Harethaknutr, Wulfbert and Godric. But the church was also represented and three of the Twelve were priests, including Siward and Halfdan. The political strength of the original elite is clear as by 1086, the time of the Domesday Book, all but two of these positions were still in the hands of men with Anglo-Danish names.

ARTIST'S IMPRESSION OF A NORMAN SHIP F6019

The greater landholders, however, did not fair so well. One of these was Tochi, son of Outi, who possessed a hall, at least thirty messuages, or houses, and two churches. By 1086 Tochi's estate had in the main passed into the hands of Geoffrey Alselin, a Norman. Other important Norman landholders included Gilbert of Gant, Countess Judith and Bishop Remigius. So while the existing Anglo-Danish elite may have largely retained the day-to-day running of the city, its commerce and affairs, the new Norman elite gradually appropriated the property they and others had owned.

Perhaps the greatest appropriation of property under the new regime was by the king himself and associated with the creation of the castle. The Anglo-Saxon Chronicle tells us that a castle was established at Lincoln in 1068, following a rising in the north that King William was forced to suppress. It is clear from both Domesday Book and archaeological evidence that the earliest Norman 'castle' comprised the entire upper walled city. It is likely that a castle motte, or raised mound of earth, was hurriedly thrown up in the south-west corner of the upper city, on the site of the present day Lucy Tower. The area outside of the motte would therefore have been assigned as the castle bailey, an identity that has held down through the ages in the area known as 'the Bail'.

One of the earliest constables of the castle was a man named Robert de la Haye; the de la Hayes continued to hold the office of constable for a further century, some of the most troubled in the castle's history. The

Medieval and Later Lincoln

CASTLE GATEWAY 1890 25670

A HISTORY & CELEBRATION

castle as we recognise it today, with its curtain wall, east and west gates, western motte, and inner bailey, was built at the beginning of the 12th century. It is thought the western and northern elements of this castle wall were constructed first, including the massive bank and ditch – now filled in – which can best be viewed from Westgate.

Another figure of significance in the city was the sheriff, who represented the king. The earliest known sheriff was Thorold, who passed the title to his niece, Countess Lucy de Taillebois. She was a truly remarkable woman who outlived three husbands, at which point the king was persuaded that his best course of action was to allow her to hold the title without re-marriage. It was probably around the time of her death in 1136 that the wooden keep on the original motte was rebuilt in stone, and became known for evermore as the Lucy Tower.

Lucy's sons played a direct part in Lincoln's involvement in the troubled middle years of the 12th century and the civil wars of Stephen and Matilda. The two brothers, Ranulf and William, were powerful members of the nobility who held lordship over as much as a third of the kingdom. In the winter of 1140 they were said to have taken control of the castle in true cloak and dagger style. They first sent their wives to pay a social call on the wife of the constable, then used this subterfuge to

THE CASTLE 1906 55111

A view of the Observatory Tower from inside the castle walls, the great mound of earth or motte can clearly be seen heaped against the base of the tower.

MEDIEVAL AND LATER LINCOLN

gain entry to the castle for themselves and their men-at-arms.

Having taken the castle Ranulph set about reinforcing it; the motte and keep in the south-east corner of the site, now known as the Observatory Tower, may well date to this time or soon after. In desperation the citizens of Lincoln appealed to their king, and Stephen came with an army to besiege the fortress. It is said he attacked the castle by placing bowmen and siege engines on the west front of the cathedral. A relieving rebel army, led by Matilda's illegitimate half-brother Robert, Earl of Gloucester, arrived in February 1141 and approached the castle from the west.

The king's army, supported by the loyal inhabitants of the city, joined battle with the rebels. Unfortunately the king's troops were easily overwhelmed, and despite fighting heroically with a Danish battle-axe given him by a Lincoln citizen, Stephen was captured. This short battle became famous as the 'Joust of Lincoln'. In the aftermath the city was sacked and many of its inhabitants killed. Escorted to Bristol, Stephen was later freed in exchange for Earl Robert who was himself seized at a later date. It was not until 1126 that Stephen finally forced Ranulph to surrender the castle. In celebration the king decided to observe the Christmas festivities in Lincoln, boldly wearing his crown in defiance of a superstitious rhyme that suggested,

> 'The first crowned head that enters
>   Lincoln's walls
> His reign proves stormy and his
>   kingdom falls.'

Fact File

The Lucy Tower

There were two medieval towers in Lincoln called 'Lucy'. The original was the Lucy tower keep within the castle, named after Countess Lucy de Taillebois. The other was a small tower built as part of the later city defences on the Brayford waterfront. This was excavated in 1972 and dates to the late 13th century. Why it was also called the Lucy tower we do not know.

While the castle dominates the south-west corner of the upper city the south-east portion belongs to the great cathedral. Almost immediately after the Norman Conquest Wulfwig Bishop of Dorchester, within whose diocese Lincoln was located, died. To fill the vacancy William turned to the almoner of the abbey of Fécamp in Normandy, one of his original supporters. Thus Remigius became the first Norman bishop in England.

After removing his seat from Dorchester to Lincoln, and placing it literally in St Mary's Church in the south-east corner of the upper city, Remigius asked the king for permission to build a great new cathedral. William granted his request in 1072 and immediately the Bail echoed with the sound of masons and labourers building the new edifice, a sound that would both offend and delight the ears of those who dwelt in this part of the city for much of the following 200 years.

LINCOLN, AERIAL VIEW FROM SOUTH-WEST c1960 L49088

A HISTORY & CELEBRATION

The first cathedral was a simple affair constructed in a traditional Norman style. The block-like fortified palace building of Remigius ingeniously formed the west front; behind this the nave extended some 100 metres east, ending just short of the city wall. If one takes a view of the magnificent west front seen today, the rough ashlar stones of the earliest structure with its three round-arched doorways can still be seen framed clearly within the later more elaborate façade. The cathedral founded by Bishop Remigius was completed and consecrated in 1092, the year of his death.

The life of the cathedral revolved around prayer and worship but there were also the widely scattered estates of the diocese to administer; thus a considerable staff came to be associated with the cathedral and its surroundings. Many of these individuals and

THE FRIEZE ON THE WEST FRONT

12TH CENTURY FRIEZE ON THE WEST FRONT OF THE CATHEDRAL 2004 L49704k (Craig Spence)

Early medieval cathedrals were visual marvels adorned with colourful carvings and painted panels. Such images allowed the majority, who could neither read nor write, to understand the teachings of the Bible. In the 12th century the west front of Lincoln cathedral was adorned with a frieze that depicted graphic scenes from the Old Testament. Designed to instil fear and obedience, several of the panels show the punishments suffered in Hell by those who have committed deadly sins. There are also happier images of Abraham, the Elect in Heaven, and Noah and the Flood. The carvings have deteriorated much over the centuries and have recently undergone several years of careful restoration.

MEDIEVAL AND LATER LINCOLN

CATHEDRAL 1890 25626

their families were housed in buildings in the surrounding streets, leading to the formation of a cathedral precinct or close. But all was not peaceful within the close; in the same year as the 'Joust of Lincoln', 1141, the cathedral suffered the first in a series of disasters. A fire swept through the building, possibly during the riotous aftermath of the battle, destroying the timber roof. The restoration was in the hands of Bishop Alexander 'The Magnificent' who, introducing the most up-to-date Romanesque architectural style, enlarged the west front and initiated the building of the two western towers.

Within a few decades much of the bold architecture of Bishop Alexander was found wanting, particularly the use of stone vaulting within the body of the church. In 1185 an earthquake rocked the upper city and the cathedral came crashing down. Only the west front seems to have escaped significant damage. Recovering from such a disaster would require the energy and dynamism of a rare individual; Lincoln needed a miracle and only a saint could deliver one. As luck would have it such a saint was to be found, in the person of Hugh of Avalon, a Carthusian monk, who arrived in Lincoln as its new bishop the following year.

Bishop Hugh was a charismatic man of great compassion; his care for the sick and the poor was renowned. What is more, he had no fear of his king, Henry II, whom he defied at regular intervals. But Bishop Hugh's greatest contribution was the rebuilding of the cathedral in the glorious gothic style we see today.

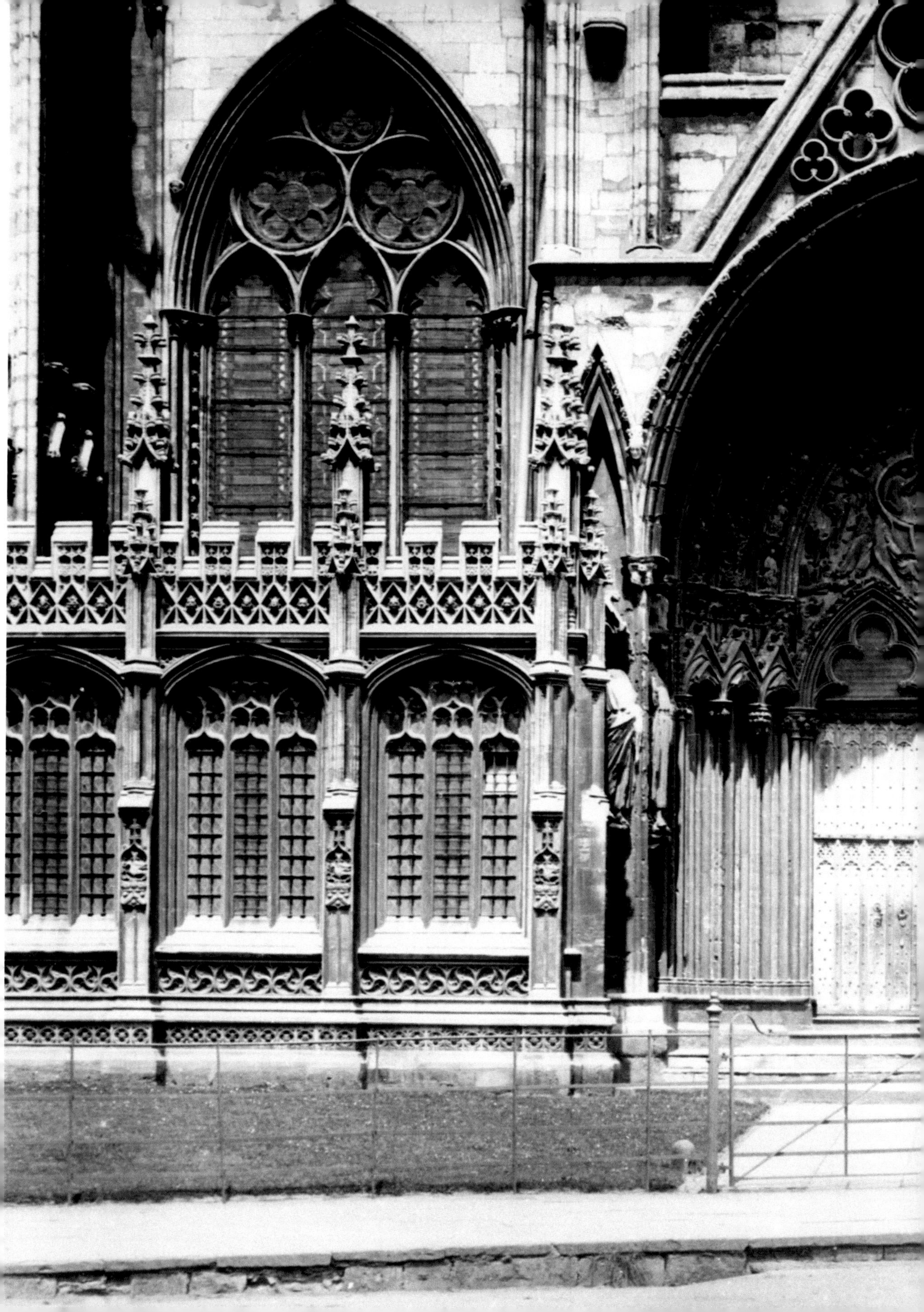

CATHEDRAL, SOUTH PORCH 1895 35547

A HISTORY & CELEBRATION

Hugh decided to extend the cathedral eastward; to do so he had to break through the city wall. The new east end of the cathedral, the choir, was of a complex design of multiple apsidal chapels that extended across the city ditch. Though it no longer exists, the line of its walls can be traced in markings set in the floor of the present-day Angel choir.

Bishop Hugh did not live to see his new cathedral finished; he died in 1200 in London. His body was brought back to Lincoln for burial; there King John and King William of Scotland, three archbishops and many others met it. With little delay he was canonised in 1220. Then came another disaster; in 1239 the inhabitants of the Bail and Close had to run for shelter as, through a failing in its design, the massive central tower came tumbling down.

It was during the 11th and 12th centuries that Lincoln was perhaps at its height as a centre of commerce. Its wharves, merchant's houses and markets bustled with life and wealth, a wealth principally built on the wool trade and the making of woollen cloth. Medieval Lincoln produced a fine range of cloths; its best and most expensive was known as scarlet, but there was also blanket, which was white, and two varieties known as say; grey and green. It is the green say that is meant when we think of 'Lincoln green' today, usually in the context of Robin Hood and his Merry Men!

Among the wealthiest of the merchants were a number who dwelt in the Wigford suburb. Here there was space for prosperous individuals to build substantial houses complete with suitable outbuildings. In the same area the Great Guild of St Mary had their hall. St Mary's Guildhall was built during the 1150s, or soon after, as a private residence on a palatial scale. Later it was acquired by the Gild as their meeting place. The building still stands today on the eastern side of the lower High Street; it is currently occupied by the Lincoln Civic Trust. Two fortified gates marked the southern boundary of the suburb, and in a sense Lincoln as a whole: Little Bargate and Great Bargate. Beyond lay the important religious precinct of the Gilbertine Priory of St Katherine, founded around the same time the Guildhall was constructed.

ST MARY'S GUILDHALL 2004 ZZZ01601 (Zoe Tomlinson)

Medieval and Later Lincoln

JEW'S HOUSE 1890 25664

There are other important stone-built residences from this date in the city proper. At the top of Steep Hill is one named Norman House. This was once thought to have been the home of Aaron of Lincoln, a hugely wealthy Jewish financier who lent money to kings, barons and bishops, but prior to his death in 1185 he actually lived in the Bail. Further downhill, on the Strait, is another stone-built house, this time more closely associated with Lincoln's important Jewish community. Appropriately named 'Jew's House', it was owned by a Jewish woman named Bellaset in the late 13th century, shortly before the expulsion of the entire Jewish community from England in 1290.

Two other structures of note from this period are the Bishops' Palace, constructed in the shadow of the cathedral, and High Bridge just to the south of the Stonebow. The Bishops' Palace was begun properly in the 1150s, but was greatly rebuilt by Bishop Hugh after 1185. Perched on a terrace below the upper city wall it comprised an east and west hall with adjoining chambers and kitchens. Now in the care of English Heritage, the ruinous site is an evocative reminder of the political power once wielded by the nation's highest clerics.

High Bridge dates from the 12th century; replacing an earlier ford it spanned the River Witham. The earliest element of the bridge can be seen in the vaulting beneath the

39

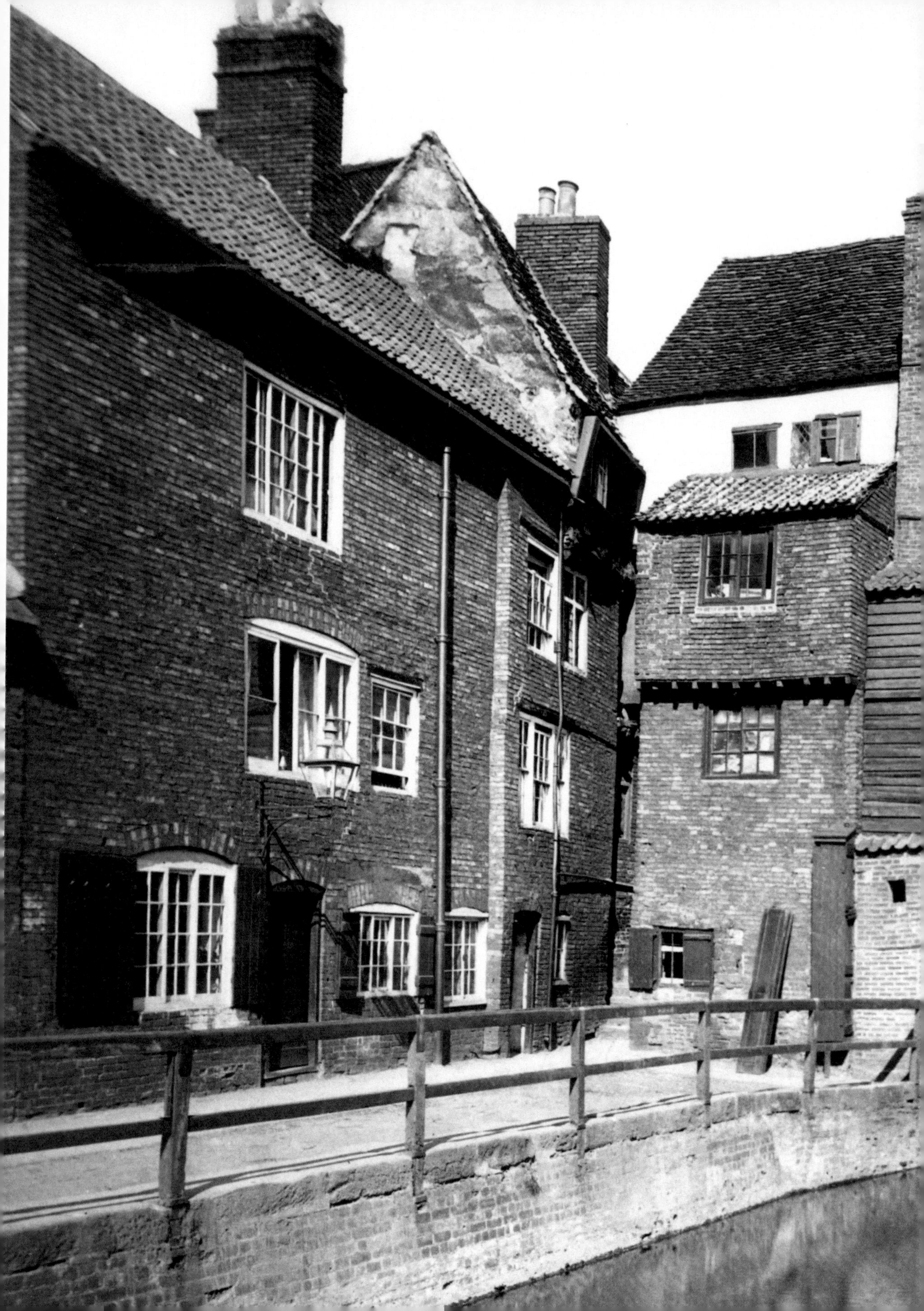

HIGH BRIDGE 1890 25659

An interesting view of the rear of the buildings on High Bridge, taken before major restoration work was carried out in 1901.

A HISTORY & CELEBRATION

structure. The bridge was enlarged following the murder of Thomas à Becket, archbishop of Canterbury, to allow the construction of a chapel dedicated to St Thomas. Later, in the 16th century, High Bridge gained buildings on its western side. Although a common feature of later medieval bridges the survival of these structures into the present day is unique in England.

If we return to the 13th century for a moment we can consider Lincoln Castle's second great medieval conflict. King John came to the throne in 1189 but he was soon at loggerheads with his barons. This discontent culminated in 1215 with the signing of the Magna Carta at Runnymede. Only four original 'copies' of this most important of political documents survive; one is in Lincoln. The Lincoln Magna Carta probably belonged to the bishop, Hugh of Wells, who was at Runnymede. It is currently displayed in the castle.

King John was not, however, about to honour his side of Magna Carta. The barons in desperation turned to Louis, Dauphin of France, who sent troops to England; they laid siege to Lincoln Castle. The constable of the castle was a formidable woman named Nicholaa de la Haye, and she at first bought them off, but after John's death at Newark in October 1216 the French returned and took over the city for the rebels. William the Marshal, defending the rights of the child king Henry III, gathered an army and early in 1217 marched on Lincoln.

While some troops entered the castle by the western gate, the main force battled their way into the city through the Newport Arch. Within a short space of time the French troops were in retreat as the fighting raged through the Bail, down the High Street, and out into the Wigford suburb. Afterwards the city and inhabitants suffered greatly for their support of

THE CASTLE, COBB HALL 2004 L49705k (Craig Spence)

the rebel cause, an event that became known as the 'Battle of Lincoln Fair'.

A new tower, named Cobb Hall, was added to the castle defences following the battle of 1217. The tower roof was probably used as a platform for a great crossbow or catapult, while the floors below contained dungeons for prisoners

The city gradually recovered and by the 1230s was playing host to several new orders of religious establishment, the friaries. The orders of the Grey Friars, Dominicans, Austin Friars and the Friars of the Sack all built houses in Lincoln. Of these the only surviving structure is the infirmary hall of the Grey Friars, sandwiched between Free School Lane

Medieval and Later Lincoln

and Broadgate. To the east of the city a smaller establishment belonged to the Black Monks of St Mary of York. A few ruinous remnants of this cell still survive in a park setting on the south side of Monks Road, from which the name derives.

In the 13th century the cathedral underwent further restoration. First the central tower was rebuilt and then the masons turned their tools towards the east end of the church where they pulled down most of St Hugh's Choir. It was replaced with the larger and more regular Angel Choir, named after the figures of angels that look down from the spandrels of the arcades. In 1280 St Hugh's tomb was, with great ceremony, relocated to the new Choir where with the addition of a golden casket containing the saint's head it became a shrine for pilgrimage. A deep groove can still be seen in the stone paving before the shrine where the toes of hundreds of thousands of pilgrims rubbed as they knelt to pray.

Among the congregation present at the translation of St Hugh's remains were King Edward I and Queen Eleanor. Their marriage, though of political origins, soon turned to one of deep love and lasting affection. In 1290 Eleanor was taken ill and died at Harby, close to Lincoln. Her body was brought to the priory of St Katherine's to the south of the city. She was then embalmed, and while her body began its journey to London and burial in Westminster Abbey her internal organs were entombed in Lincoln cathedral.

MONKS ABBEY 1890 25667

A HISTORY & CELEBRATION

THE LINCOLN IMP

The builders of the shrine of St Hugh wanted pilgrims to have in mind the ever-present danger of evil, so they included a reminder of the devil within the Angel Choir. A carving, in the form of a small diabolical creature, was placed high above the left shoulder of pilgrims as they knelt to pray. The creature has become world-famous as 'The Lincoln Imp'. There are many fanciful stories about the imp; perhaps the most popular is that the imp was having so much fun causing trouble in the cathedral that the angels turned him to stone, although other stories seem to emphasise that he was blown into the cathedral during a tremendous storm. Whatever the myths, the imp has become a symbol of Lincoln, especially after it was popularised as a tourist item during the Victorian period. In fact James Usher, jeweller and founder of the Usher Gallery, was said to have made much of his wealth by selling replicas of the imp!

THE LINCOLN IMP c1955 L49078

The famous Eleanor Crosses marked the route to London. Lincoln's, situated at the bottom of Cross O' Cliff Hill, was taken down during the 17th century, though a small rediscovered fragment is displayed in the castle grounds.

Kings Edward I, II and III summoned parliaments to Lincoln in 1301, 1316 and 1327, respectively. Such parliaments met in the chapter house of the cathedral, which together with other buildings lay within the boundaries of the Close. During the early 14th century a fortified wall and gates were constructed around that area. Today several stretches of the wall remain, though the only sizeable elements of the gates are Exchequergate, which faces the west front, and Pottergate at the junction with Lindum Road.

A council made up of the greater men of Lincoln governed the wider medieval city, and from 1206 there was also a mayor. At the end of the 14th century the city council began to meet in a chamber above the Stonebow. The modern city council still sits at the Stonebow

Medieval and Later Lincoln

and is called to each meeting by the ringing of the Mote bell, which dates from 1371. The city's rights and status were reaffirmed in 1386 when Richard II presented a sword of state, an item still proudly in the city's possession.

But Lincoln was above all else a market town. The citizens jealously guarded their trading privileges, privileges that made several very wealthy indeed. Lincoln merchants traded far and wide, having shops in London or Winchester and ships in the great medieval port of Boston at the seaward end of the Witham. The significance of the Lincoln market resulted in the grant of the staple to the city in 1326, meaning that all wool, hides, skins and other produce had to pass through the city before export. Yet if receiving the staple was a reflection of Lincoln's trading strength, the loss of the staple to Boston in 1369 signalled the beginning of the end for the city's commerce.

CATHEDRAL, NORTH-EAST 1923 74644

Sited to the north of the cathedral is the circular chapter house. The building was used as a venue for parliament in the early 14th century.

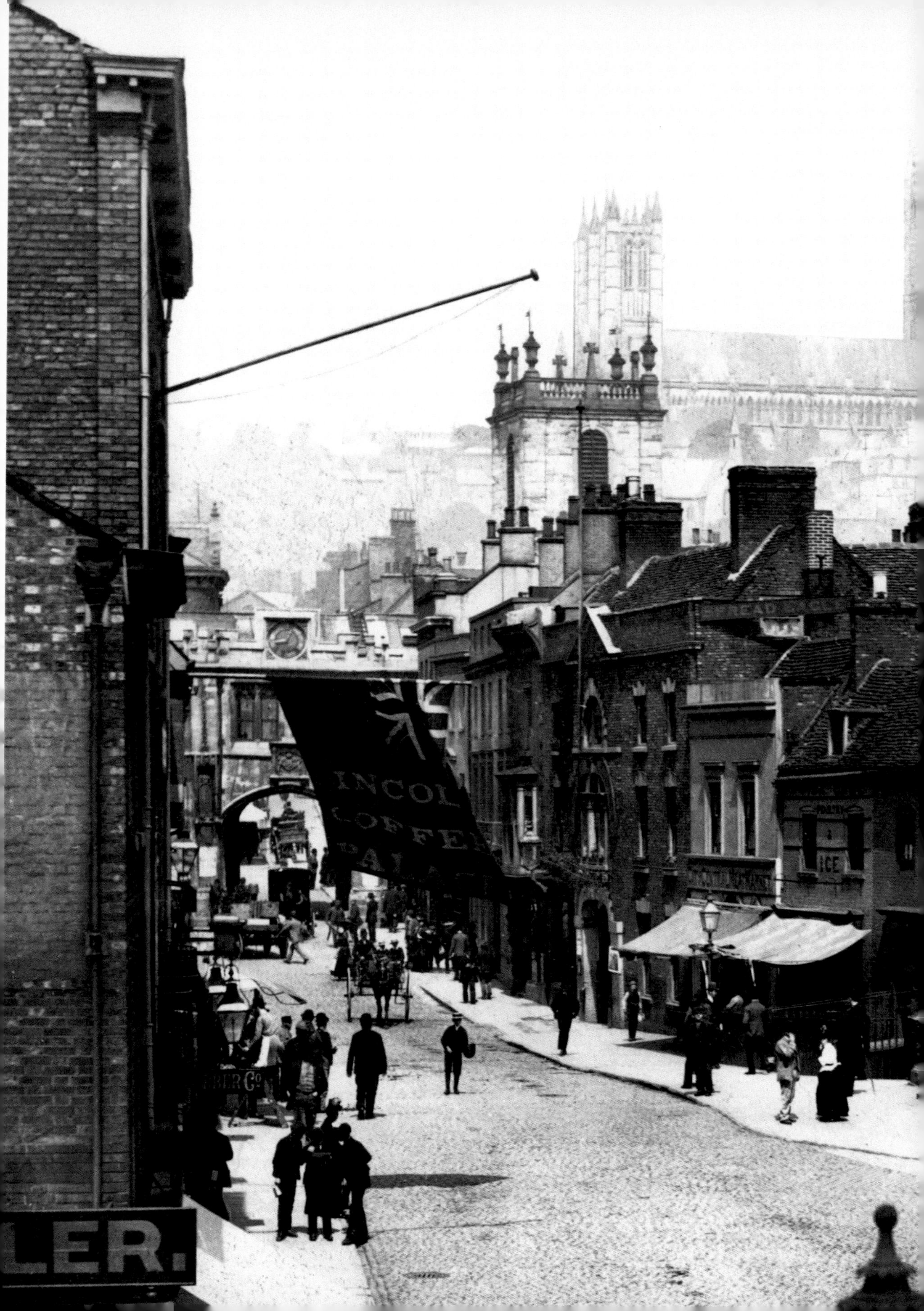
LER.
ICE

THE CATHEDRAL AND STONEBOW 1890 25654

A History & Celebration

POTTERGATE AND CATHEDRAL 1890 25656

Despite some efforts to reorganise the government of the city and to gain relief from various taxes, Lincoln during the 14th century was a city of past glories. Not only the economy suffered as the wool trade collapsed, but in 1439 the Black Death decimated the people themselves. We have no general mortality figure for the epidemic but we do know that nearly two thirds of the city's clergy died. Many of the survivors fell into debt and destitution. The fabric of the city gradually decayed, city walls and gates lay unrepaired and crumbling, and the vacant properties – including churches – were cleared and not rebuilt. By 1524 Lincoln, once the 3rd city of the kingdom, had slipped to a weak 19th place.

The early 16th century saw the rise of an indomitable Tudor king, Henry VIII. Henry's attack on the church of the day was resented in many parts, and in none more so than Lincolnshire. In 1536 the commons of Lincolnshire rose in rebellion; some 40,000 men converged on Lincoln in an attempt to end Henry's plan to reform the church and dissolve the monasteries. Within two weeks the rising was over and the commons dispersed. The arrival of a royal army saw to that.

MEDIEVAL AND LATER LINCOLN

In due course the dissolution of the monastic houses and friaries took place. The cathedral suffered in 1542 when its treasure was confiscated and its shrines destroyed, including that of St Hugh. In all some 74 kilos of gold and 121 kilos of silver were seized. The cathedral treasurer was so disgusted that he threw his keys to the ground saying 'so ceaseth the office of treasurer'; to this day Lincoln cathedral has no treasurer. If pious observers desired a sign of God's displeasure they undoubtedly believed they had one six years later. During a ferocious storm the great spire which since 1311 had crowned the cathedral's central tower disintegrated and fell to the ground. The cathedral's two-century reign as the world's highest structure had come to a sudden dramatic end.

But it was not only the Crown that envied the possessions of the church. The city fathers also had an eye on the prize. For many years the city had a concern to provide a plentiful supply of water to the inhabitants. Now was their chance. In 1539 the city took possession of the monastic conduits. As a result two new conduit heads, stone-covered water tanks, were built: one near High Bridge, the other outside St Mary-le-Wigford. The latter was constructed of ornate stone taken from the nearby Carmelite friary; it still stands to the west of the church.

At the beginning of the 17th century various attempts were made to halt Lincoln's seemingly relentless decline. One focus of attention was the overgrown and silted up Fossdyke, the waterway that connected Lincoln to the Trent. If it were to be of use for commercial transport it would need cleaning and dredging. The project to do so was beset by difficulties from all sides – financial, political, social and practical – and had little lasting impact on the watercourse itself.

Things looked up briefly for the city when King James I paid an extended visit in 1617. He was entertained with hunting and horse racing on the heath to the south of Lincoln, cockfighting at the George by the Stonebow and fencing at the Spread Eagle. In 1642 his son Charles I also visited the city, but not for pleasure. The king had been forced to leave London by the menaces of parliament; he travelled to Hull where he was turned away, after which he passed through Lincoln. While a great crowd was said to have greeted him they did not rush to his cause, indeed by this time the city was largely in the control of

Fact File

Catherine Swynford

One of the most famous historical novels ever written was partly set in Lincoln. Anya Seton's 1954 historical romance 'Katherine' (inaccurately spelt with a K!) is based on the extraordinary life of Catherine Swynford.

Catherine became mistress to John of Gaunt, son of Edward III, and was mother to four of his children. One of these was John Beaufort from whom all of England's succeeding royal families can be traced. She died in 1405 and is buried in Lincoln Cathedral.

A HISTORY & CELEBRATION

> ## Fact File
>
> ### Henry VIII and Catherine Howard
>
> *In 1541 King Henry VIII visited Lincoln, accompanied by Catherine Howard, his fifth wife. The citizens received him with great ceremony – the city council granted themselves new outfits for the occasion, and he then visited the cathedral. Afterwards he stayed overnight at the Bishops' Palace as a guest of Bishop Longland. It was later claimed one of the adulterous incidents used to condemn the queen occurred during that interlude.*

puritan councillors and ministers, though they had wisely stayed away.

During the ensuing Civil War Lincoln found itself in a difficult position. Sandwiched between the parliamentarian south and the royalist north, the city changed hands on several occasions. Initially a royalist force garrisoned the town; however following the battle of Winceby in 1643 Lincoln surrendered to the advancing parliamentarian army of the Earl of Manchester. For five months Manchester's troops over-wintered in the Castle, Bail and Close, whilst the earl's headquarters were established at the Angel Inn on the corner of Eastgate and Bailgate. In March 1644 the earl was forced to retreat, surrendering the city to a larger royalist force brought up by Prince Rupert.

However, Rupert was needed elsewhere so, leaving a small garrison, he departed for Oxford. It was not long before Manchester returned to besiege the city, this time with Cromwell for support. On 3 May the assault began. Storming the city from the south Manchester's troops made steady progress into the upper city and castle, though heavy rain delayed their attack. As the earl reported, the attack faltered: it 'being so slippery it was not possible for our Foot to crawl up the hill … being near as steep as the eaves of a house.' In the early hours of the morning on 6 May the final assault commenced. Within little more than fifteen minutes the battle was over. Lincoln was parliamentarian again.

The upper city and cathedral close were then pillaged by the victorious troops. They particularly focused on religious buildings and statuary, ripping the brasses from the floor of the cathedral, despoiling the ancient tombs; they raided the houses of the Close and all but destroyed the Deanery adjacent to the west front. In the following days and weeks lead and timber were stripped from many of the city's churches and the open shells plundered for their stone by both soldier and citizen alike. The activities became so frenzied that in June the Commons were forced to issue an order forbidding the removal of lead or bells not only from churches but also houses within the city of Lincoln.

Lincoln suffered one further episode of conflict in 1648, during the Second Civil War. A large force of royalist troops attacked the small parliamentary garrison. With the castle slighted and undefendable the garrison

MEDIEVAL AND LATER LINCOLN

retreated into the Bishops' Palace. During the short siege the palace somehow caught fire. The garrison surrendered but the damage was done. The bulk of the palace complex would never be rebuilt.

By the end of the 17th century Lincoln had a population of little more than 3,000 individuals. It was still the seat of both secular and ecclesiastical government but its economy had never been weaker. Buildings throughout the city were decayed and derelict. In 1712 Daniel Defoe visited Lincoln which he describe as 'an ancient, ragged, and still decaying city; so full of the ruins of monasteries and religious houses, that the very barns, stables and hog-sties were built church-fashion, with stone walls, arched windows and doors…'

Some new buildings were being constructed, however, or at least rebuilding in a new style was under way. The Bail, and the Close in particular, quickly recovered and several fine early 18th century buildings are to be found lining its streets. In the lower city recovery was slower but in 1689 the changes that had recently occurred in religious practice were made manifest when the Quakers constructed their Meeting House in Park Street. The cottage-like building still stands, though much changed in outward appearance.

The 18th century was a period of increasing urban gentility throughout England; towns competed to be seen as orderly and civilised, and why should the inhabitants of Lincoln be thought of any differently? One of the first steps in this direction came with the

ST MARY'S CHURCH AND CONDUIT 1890 25661

A HISTORY & CELEBRATION

THE GUILDHALL 1890 25657

MEDIEVAL AND LATER LINCOLN

construction of the Butter Market in 1736, north of the Stonebow. It was adjacent to the church of St Peter-at-Arches, itself rebuilt in 1724. The stone-built covered market was funded from the proceeds of a decade of civic banquets. But such 'improvement' was not always welcomed. Just ten years earlier a mob of 500 had gathered outside the cathedral to oppose a plan to take down the spires that still graced the western towers. The plan was abandoned allowing the spires another 82 years of life before their removal produced the Lincoln Cathedral skyline that we see today.

Lincoln attracted provincial gentry who demanded entertainment. Aside from the regular race meetings that took place on Lincoln Heath, there were theatrical performances and social functions. Lincoln's first theatre was constructed for William Herbert's Company of Comedians at the Harlequin Inn near the top of Steep Hill in 1744. The theatre moved south to the High Street later in the century but the Harlequin still stands, though it served its last drink in 1931; today it is a bookshop.

Georgian high society required a formal meeting place and one was opened in 1745 on the east side of Bailgate. The Assembly Rooms became the pride of the upper city social elite. The building, containing one of the finest Georgian interiors in Lincoln, still exists but is now concealed behind a municipal entrance block built in 1914. Not to be outdone the commercial elite of the lower city built their own assembly rooms.

A HISTORY & CELEBRATION

STEEP HILL c1950 L49020

Medieval and Later Lincoln

THE LAWN 2004 ZZZ01602 (Zoe Tomlinson)

These were completed in 1757 and were located above the Butter Market.

The medical sciences were also being greatly advanced during this period and in 1777 a new city hospital, with beds for 40 patients, was opened in a dominant position on the hillside just below the castle. Of wider significance was the opening of the Lincoln Lunatic Asylum, known as the Lawn, in 1820. The institution was important as it used the new 'non-restraint system' championed by Dr E P Charlesworth. This shifted the care of the mentally ill away from shackles and cells toward a more therapeutic regime.

Things were at last looking up for the city. After nearly three centuries of economic decline and physical decay the future prospects of the city seemed good. Lincoln had become the county town of a region that was to some degree benefiting from an agricultural revolution. Communications to and from the city were enhanced by improvements in the Fossdyke and Witham waterways and new buildings, both civic and private, were beginning to enhance the city's streets. The 19th century would see an even greater improvement in the fortunes of this oldest of English towns.

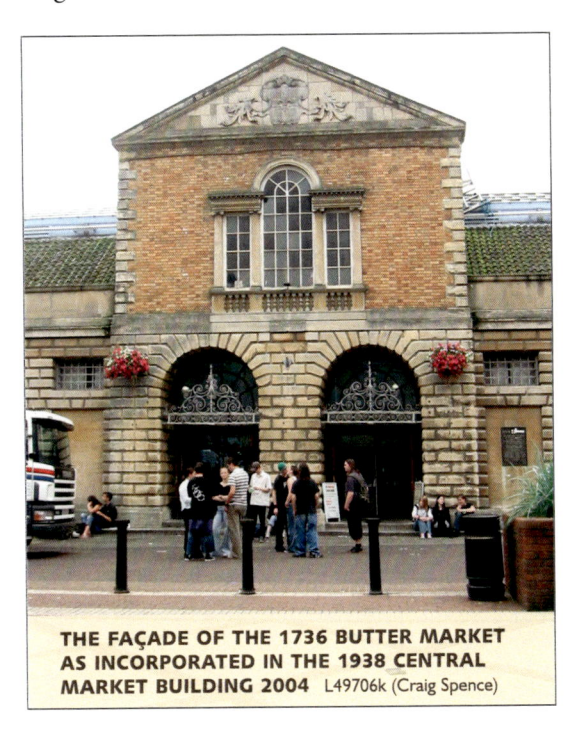

THE FAÇADE OF THE 1736 BUTTER MARKET AS INCORPORATED IN THE 1938 CENTRAL MARKET BUILDING 2004 L49706k (Craig Spence)

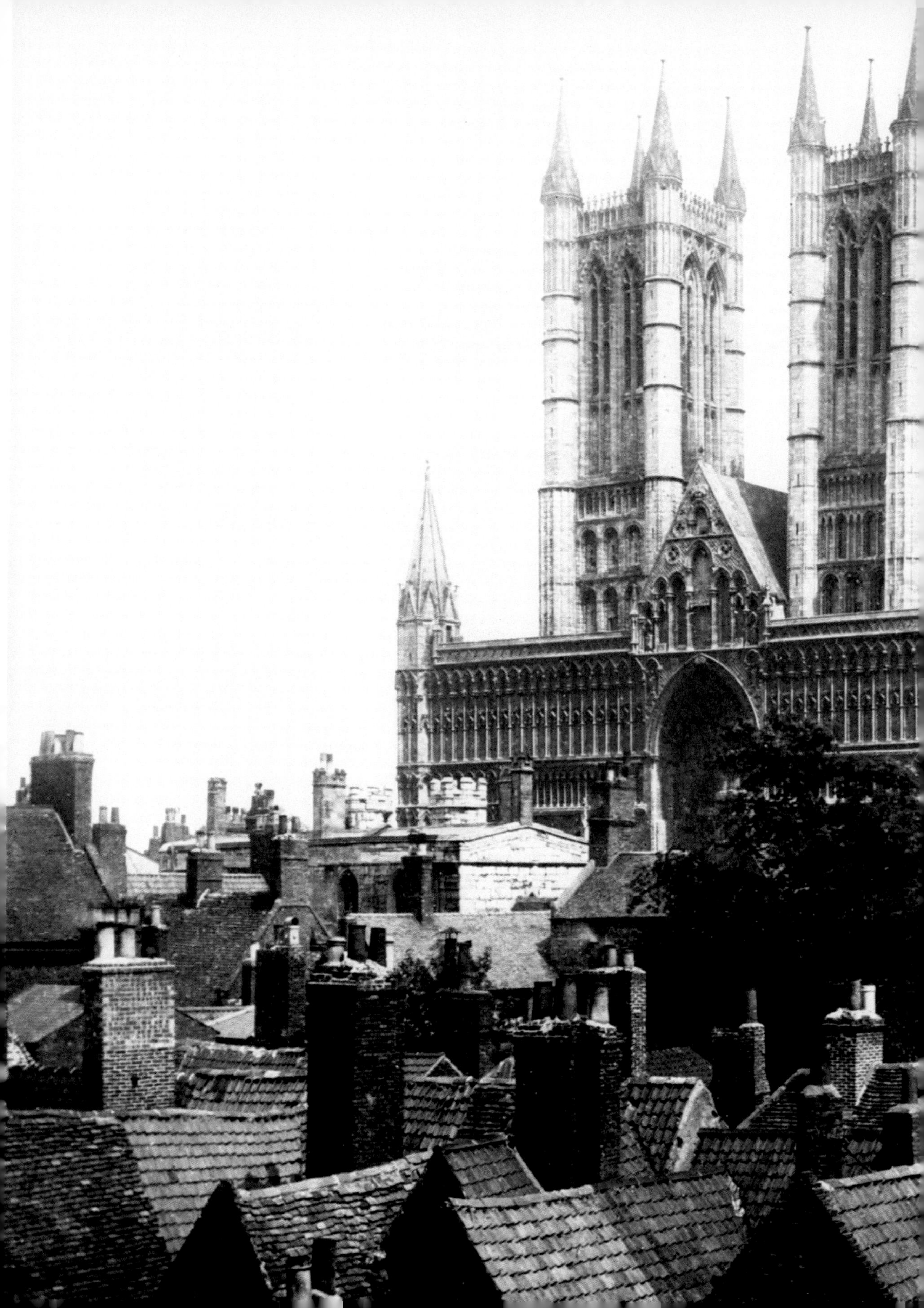

CHAPTER THREE
VICTORIAN LINCOLN

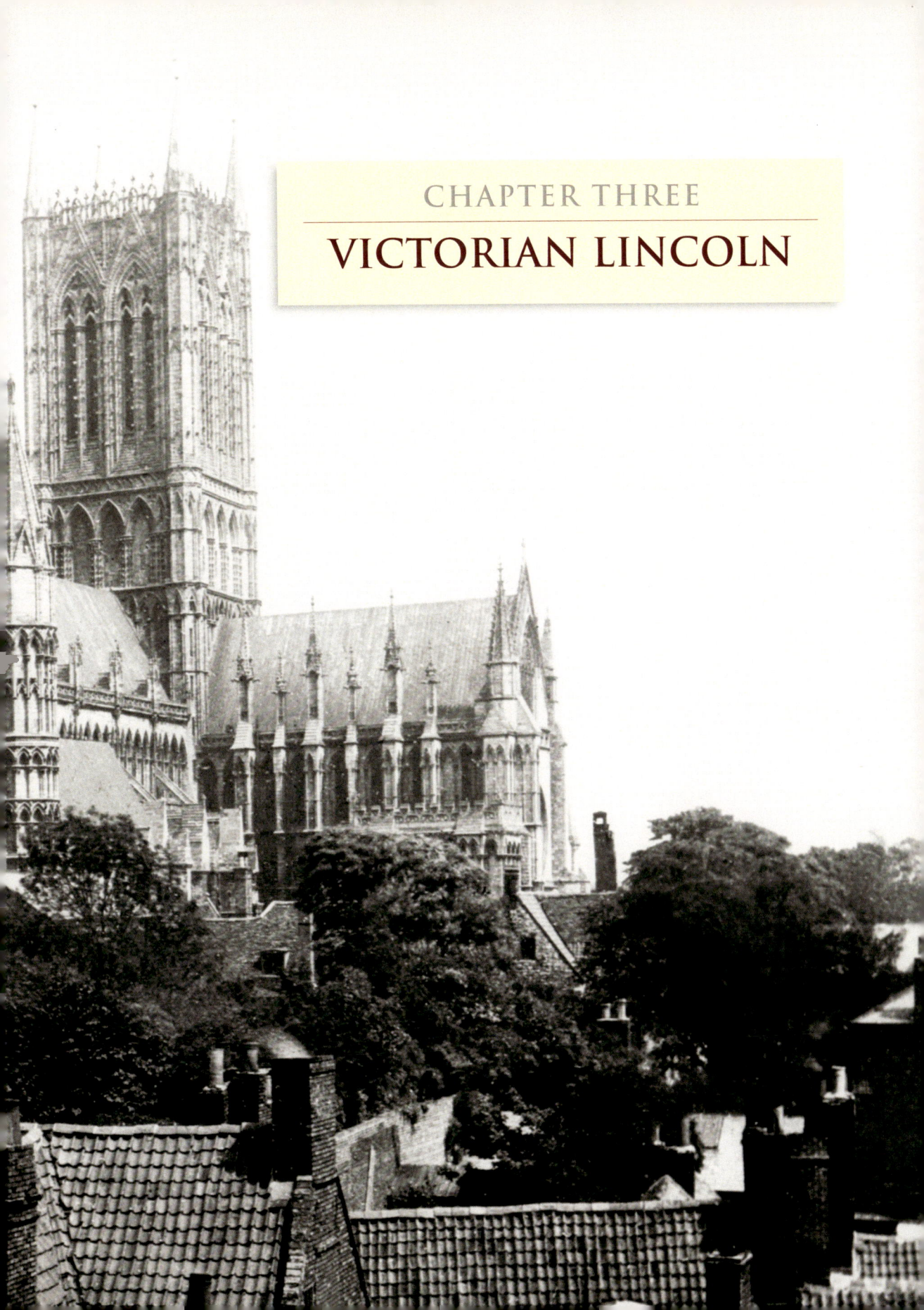

A HISTORY & CELEBRATION

BRAYFORD POOL 1890 25620

LINCOLN AT the dawn of the 19th century was a city clearly confident in its own wealth and authority, but which nonetheless had to confront increasing levels of poverty and destitution among its growing population. Commerce was alive and well, especially with the improvements carried out on the Fossdyke and Witham waterways, which helped to make Brayford Pool a working harbour once again. But it was mainly poor migrants escaping difficult conditions in the countryside that bolstered the city's population from some 7,000 in 1801 to about 8,500 in 1811.

The old poor law required parishes to care for the poor, but many parts of the city found this a difficult burden. An early attempt was made to resolve such problems in 1740, when thirteen parishes joined to open a House of Industry. This struggled on until the passing of a new poor law in 1834; as a result the Lincoln Poor Law Union was formed two years later. The Union comprised eighty-six parishes, in the city and up to ten miles distant. By 1837 a workhouse had been constructed, able to house 360 inmates.

While one institution dealt with the poor, the rich had dealings with another. In 1775 the partners of Ellison, Smith and Brown opened Lincoln's first private bank, which provided a cash service by printing its own banknotes. Another important financial institution was the trustee savings banks, which focused on the business needs of lesser tradesmen and shop-keepers, Lincoln's opened in 1816. Those without money might, however, be tempted to steal some. If they did they risked getting on the wrong side of the city constables.

Victorian Lincoln

A HISTORY & CELEBRATION

THE CASTLE 1890 25668

Those committing misdemeanours, or falling into debt, at the start of the 19th century were likely to find themselves incarcerated in the city gaol adjacent to the Stonebow. The conditions within the gaol, which consisted of two cells for debtors and a dungeon for felons, were so bad that a prison reformer described them as 'a disgrace to humanity'. They were closed in 1809, but only after a new sessions house and city gaol had been constructed at the foot of Lindum Road, itself built in 1786; the building now forms part of Lincoln College. However, Lincoln had another prison, the county gaol, located within the walls of the castle.

The county goal was built in 1787 essentially as a debtors' prison; 60 years later it was enlarged in the most notorious of fashions. An additional prison block was erected, designed for the so-called 'separate system'. Prisoners had the advantage of a single cell with running water, flush toilet and gas lighting, but were kept in total isolation. They were not allowed conversation and when taking exercise were forced to wear a leather cap, the peak of which entirely covered their faces.

It was hoped that spiritual instruction would assist convicts' moral recovery, but how could they be gathered together for a sermon while in isolation? The answer lay in the extraordinary prison chapel, designed so each prisoner occupied a single high-sided pew; they could see the minister and he could see them, but they could never see each other. The 'separate system' was

VICTORIAN LINCOLN

The two blocks of the county gaol can be seen within the castle walls on the left. The tower on the far right is Cobb Hall, which was the location of the executioner's scaffold between 1815 and 1868.

discredited in the 1850s and in 1872 prisoners were relocated to the new, and current, prison on Greetwell Road. The castle prison blocks are a remarkable survival of the Victorian criminal justice system – the chapel itself is of international importance – and they are in part open to the public.

The freer inhabitants of Lincoln also went to services, but not in the numbers their ministers would have liked. The national religious census of 1851 showed that on average only a quarter of the city's population regularly attended worship. Nevertheless the rise in Lincoln's 19th century population led to the construction or rebuilding of several churches. They included St Botolph, to the south of the city, St Nicholas on Newport (Sir Gilbert

Fact File

The Long Drop

In 1872 a cobbler from Horncastle named William Marwood carried out Britain's first 'humane' hanging in the grounds of Lincoln Castle. The self-taught executioner – he is said to have practised on sheep – perfected a system known as the 'long drop'. By determining the convict's body weight and adjusting the length of the rope, he broke the prisoner's neck and avoided a slow death by strangulation. This system continued in use until the last execution in Britain in 1965.

A HISTORY & CELEBRATION

Scott's earliest church), and the large and expensive church of St Swithin on Free School Lane (designed by James Fowler). The non-Anglican congregations were not to be outdone and in 1836 a Wesleyan chapel opened on Clasketgate. Able to seat 1,400, it became known as 'Big Wesley'. It was demolished in 1963.

Although the administration of schooling had fallen wholly on the church in earlier periods, a wider range of provision became available during the 19th century. A Lincoln Central National School opened its doors in 1813; various other educational establishments were to follow. By 1858 there were more than a hundred schools with places for some 6,000 children.

One Lincoln schoolmaster who stands out from the rest was George Boole, born in 1815 in Silver Street, the son of a shoemaker. George Boole is best known as the author of the theory of Boolean Logic and hence one of the pioneers of the modern computer age. He quickly demonstrated an aptitude for learning, especially science and mathematics. He spent his twenties working as a schoolmaster, running his own schools in Free School Lane and later on Pottergate, but also as master of the Waddington Academy. In his spare time he lectured to the Mechanics Institute then housed in the Greyfriars building. In 1849 he became Professor in Mathematics in Ireland. While there he met and married Mary Everest, niece of the explorer George Everest.

CASTLE GROUNDS c1955 L49097

In 1826 the Assize Courts building was constructed within the western half of the castle bailey; today the building remains in regular use as a crown court.

VICTORIAN LINCOLN

ART SCHOOL TO COMMUNITY COLLEGE

SCHOOL OF ART 1890 25663

In 1864 the Lincoln School of Art, founded the previous year, held the first exhibition of its students' work in a room above the Central National School in Silver Street. Moving into new premises on Monks Road in 1886, it widened its curriculum, becoming known as the School of Science and Art. Later the science teaching of the higher elementary school, originally founded by the chancellor of the cathedral, Edward Benson (later archbishop of Canterbury), also became attached to the institution and the name changed again to the Municipal Technical School. It continued to expand and was renamed as the City School in 1931. Eventually, in 1968, a move was made to new premises on Skellingthorpe Road. The school was the forerunner of today's City of Lincoln Community College, which gained the status of a specialist engineering college in 2003.

EXHIBITION OF STUDENT WORK 1864
ZZZ01590 (Lincolnshire County Council, Local Studies Collection)

A HISTORY & CELEBRATION

Never a fit man, he was caught in a rainstorm in 1864, contracted a pneumonia and died soon after. A stained glass window in the cathedral celebrates his life.

One of the biggest changes for any town during the Victorian period came with the arrival of the railway. Lincoln's first steam train rolled into the city in June 1846. The train belonged to the Midland Company and large crowds and much ceremony accompanied its arrival. The Midland Company was not, however, favoured by the city fathers as the line came from Nottingham and could only provide an indirect service to London and its lucrative agricultural and livestock markets. Instead the preferred line was that of the Great Northern Railway. While Great Northern line trains came into Lincoln Central Station, completed in 1848, the Midland Company used its own St Mark's Station a little further down the High Street. Though Lincoln St Mark's closed in the 1980s the main station building with its great Ionic portico survives, rebuilt within the new St Mark's Retail Park.

Central Station is on the eastern side of the High Street and to begin with trains ran back and forth to Lincoln via Boston and Peterborough. The line was quickly extended through to Gainsborough and Doncaster, therefore crossing the High Street. To achieve this a level crossing was installed; it is still there, making Lincoln notable as the largest English city to have the traffic along its main town centre street interrupted several times an hour by passing trains! Despite some resistance a further level crossing was installed for the trains of the Manchester, Sheffield and Lincolnshire Railway as they passed through St Mark's Station on their way to the docks at Grimsby.

A final major development came in 1882 when the Great Eastern and Great Northern companies joined forces to provide a new line that would allow Lincolnshire exports to be carried direct to the eastern counties and the port of Harwich. A third level crossing on the High Street was unthinkable so the track, known as the 'avoiding

OLD ST MARK'S STATION PORTICO 2004 L49707k (Craig Spence)

VICTORIAN LINCOLN

FROM THE HOLMES 1890 25621

line', was carried over both that road and Canwick Road on bridges. Early resistance to the railways came from those with interests in the Fossdyke and Witham waterways. In order to pacify this group the promoters of the Great Northern line undertook the purchase of the Fossdyke, offered dividends to the Witham shareholders and reduced the tolls by water generally. The monopoly gained by the railway over the waterways was soon discovered to be detrimental. As a consequence trade, and for that matter passage, along the Witham rapidly fell away, though the heavy transport capabilities of the Fossdyke and Trent route led to a partial increase in traffic. Particular victims of this change were the steam packet paddleboats that journeyed between Lincoln and Boston.

In 1842 Nathanial Clayton, a former steam packet owner, combined with his brother-in-law Joseph Shuttleworth, a boat builder, to create a foundry and engineering works south of the Witham at Stamp End. That small company, originally staffed by just 12 men, would soon become world famous as 'Clayton and Shuttleworth'. Their premises expanded rapidly and soon spread over several acres, giving employment in 1864 to some 1,400 men. The primary product of the company was highly efficient portable steam engines, which had a number of purposes, including the driving of farm machinery. Following success at the Great Exhibition in 1851 they became the largest manufacturers of steam engines and threshing machines in Britain.

THE CITY FROM CANWICK HILL 1890 25622

Looking north toward the cathedral, this view of late Victorian Lincoln is dominated by the roofs and chimneys of the numerous industrial works clustered to the south of the city.

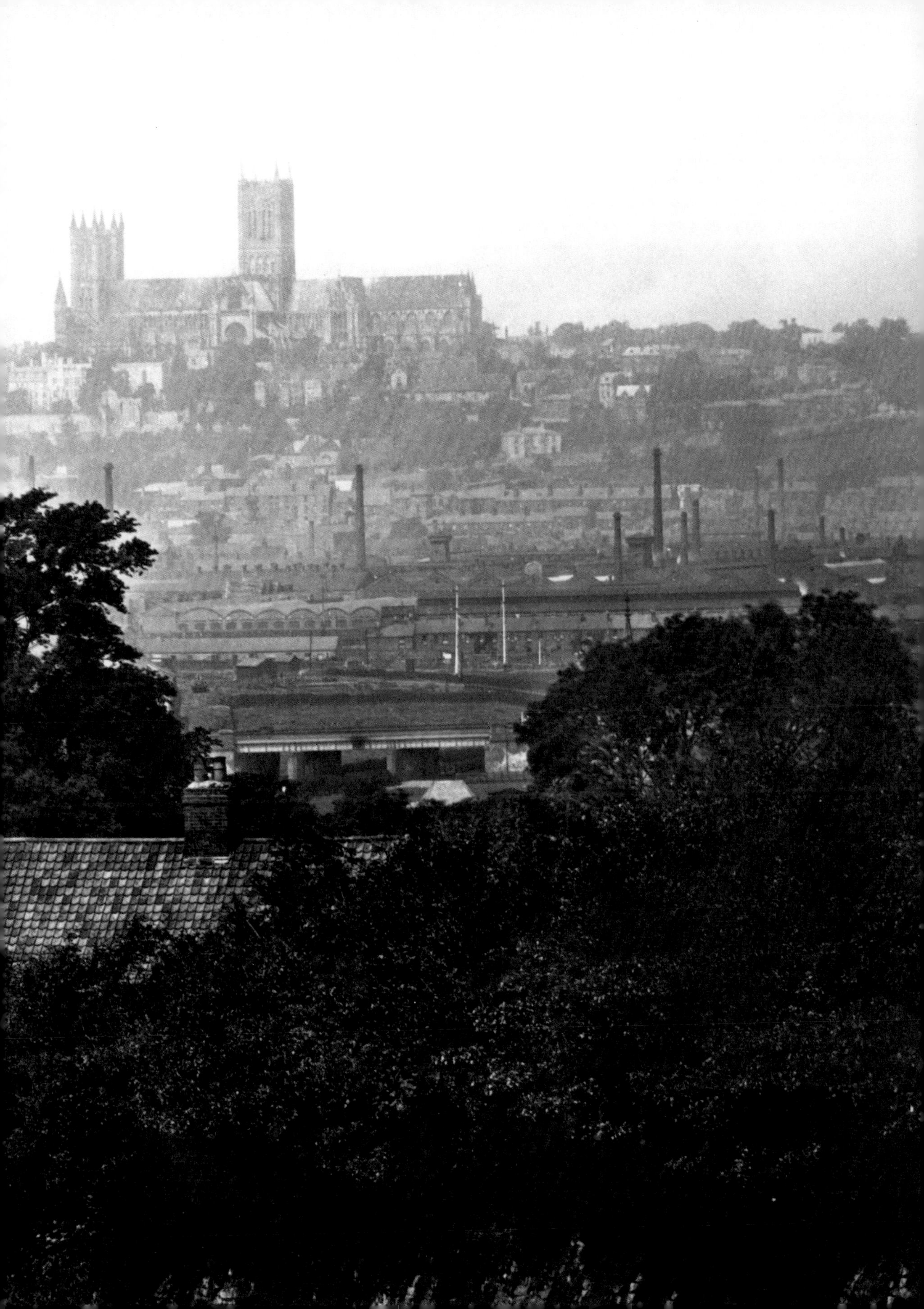

A HISTORY & CELEBRATION

Other companies soon followed; in 1851 William Foster began to supply farm machinery, Robert Robey entered the fray in 1854, but most important of all was the establishment of Proctor and Burton, joined in 1857 by Joseph Ruston. The success of Lincoln's industrialists lay mainly in their concentration on precision engineering activities. The products of Lincoln's industry flooded around the globe and several subsidiary factories were established across Europe. The impact on the population and development of Lincoln itself was no less great.

The parish of St Mary-le-Wigford housed a population of no more than 500 in 1801, but by the century's end this had grown to around 6,000, as new buildings spread across the area to house the workforce of nearby manufacturers. An even more dramatic example of the impact the new industrial works had on the growth of the city can be found in Monks Road. Here a development of artisan housing in the form of small terraced units occurred during the 1890s. In 1891 the area contained just 9 houses occupied by 43 people, but by the time of the 1901 census over 1,200 people were recorded dwelling in 269 houses. Residential development on the western side of the city at about the same time concentrated on slightly larger houses mainly destined for the aspiring middle classes. On the other hand the wealthy upper classes, which now including factory owners, chose to occupy property on the fringes of the of the city, allowing them to indulge in the construction of large villa-style houses.

Yet the city did not simply expand across the open space at its edge. Many sites within the city centre, some vacant since the 17th century, were now reoccupied. Overall Lincoln's population grew from just under 7,000 in 1801 to nearly 50,000 a century later. While housing such numbers was one issue to be faced, supplying them with food was another. There were as a result several alterations to the markets of Lincoln during the 19th century.

Lincoln's early markets had been in the streets: a corn market on Cornhill, a fish market on High Bridge, and general markets and fairs held along the High Street as far as St Mark's.

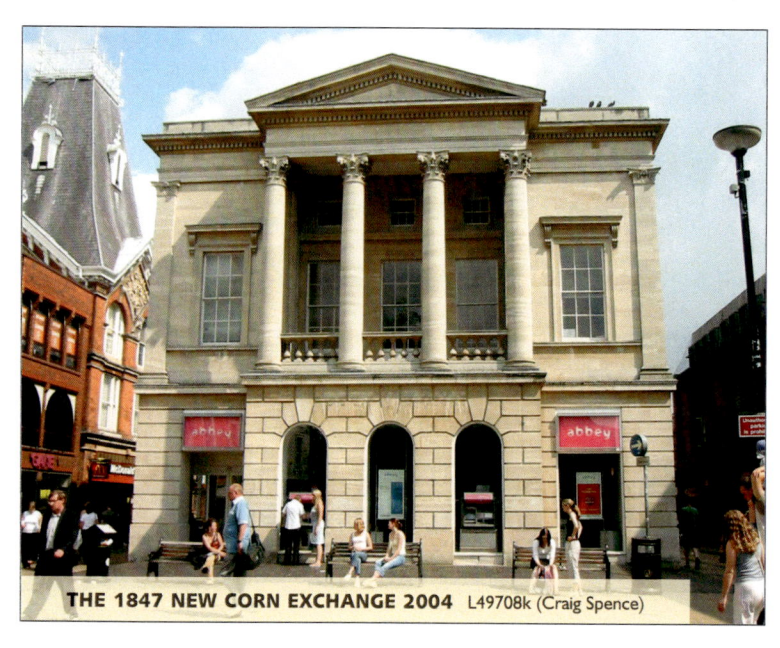

THE 1847 NEW CORN EXCHANGE 2004 L49708k (Craig Spence)

Victorian Lincoln

CATTLE MARKET AND CATHEDRAL c1950 L49043

Nonetheless there were calls to provide a new indoor facility for the corn market, but the city council were reluctant to intervene, so a private company was formed to raise the necessary capital. The foundation stone of the new Corn Exchange was laid with much pomp in 1847, the building still stands in the centre of the downhill shopping area. Just to the north is its replacement of 1879, the corn market by then having become one of the most important in the east of England.

Milling of grain and cereals was another key Lincoln industry, but in many ways one of a more traditional nature. For centuries the row of windmills that stood on the cliff edge to the west of Burton Road had been a familiar city sight. One by one these succumbed to the activities of the large steam-powered mills that lined the Witham waterside. Only one of the original windmills now remains, Ellis Mill, which was restored in 1977. One of the larger steam-powered mills was run by the Lincoln Equitable Industrial Co-operative Society, which had been formed in 1861. The Co-op became a significant commercial force within Lincoln and remains so to the present day.

The other great market development of the 19th century was that of the sheep and cattle market. Originally this was held in St Swithin's Square, just south of the Greyfriars building, but by the 1840s access to the space was too restricted and farmers and breeders called for a new site. This was found in 1849 on the north side of Monks Road; the buildings of Lincoln College now occupy the site.

A HISTORY & CELEBRATION

STONEBOW 1906 55114

VICTORIAN LINCOLN

THE ARBORETUM c1879 12496

Other markets stayed where they were. The famous Lincoln Horse Fair continued to take place annually on and around the High Street, not moving to West Common until 1929.

Many smaller traders and shopkeepers kept premises on both High Street and Sincil Street, several of those established in the 1880s and 1890s were still in business a hundred years later. Among that group is the stationer and printer J Ruddock Ltd who have been on the High Street since 1904; the company was founded in 1884 through the purchase of an older printing enterprise dating from the 1760s.

JW Ruddock like many other businessmen in Lincoln was involved in local government; others dabbled in national politics. For example in 1884 Joseph Ruston was elected as Member of Parliament for the city, however after a fierce industrial dispute he decided to retire from political life. Instead he contributed much to the city through his philanthropic activities; in 1890 he provided the Lincoln Volunteers with a new Drill Hall on Broadgate.

Fact File

Old Bread and Cheese

The great industrialist Joseph Ruston gained the somewhat mocking title of 'old bread and cheese' by claiming that the demands of workers during an industrial dispute would leave him a pauper. It did not take the people of Lincoln long to 'rename' the Drill Hall, which he had financed, as the 'Bread and Cheese Hall'.

THE CATHEDRAL AND HIGH STREET c1950 L49041

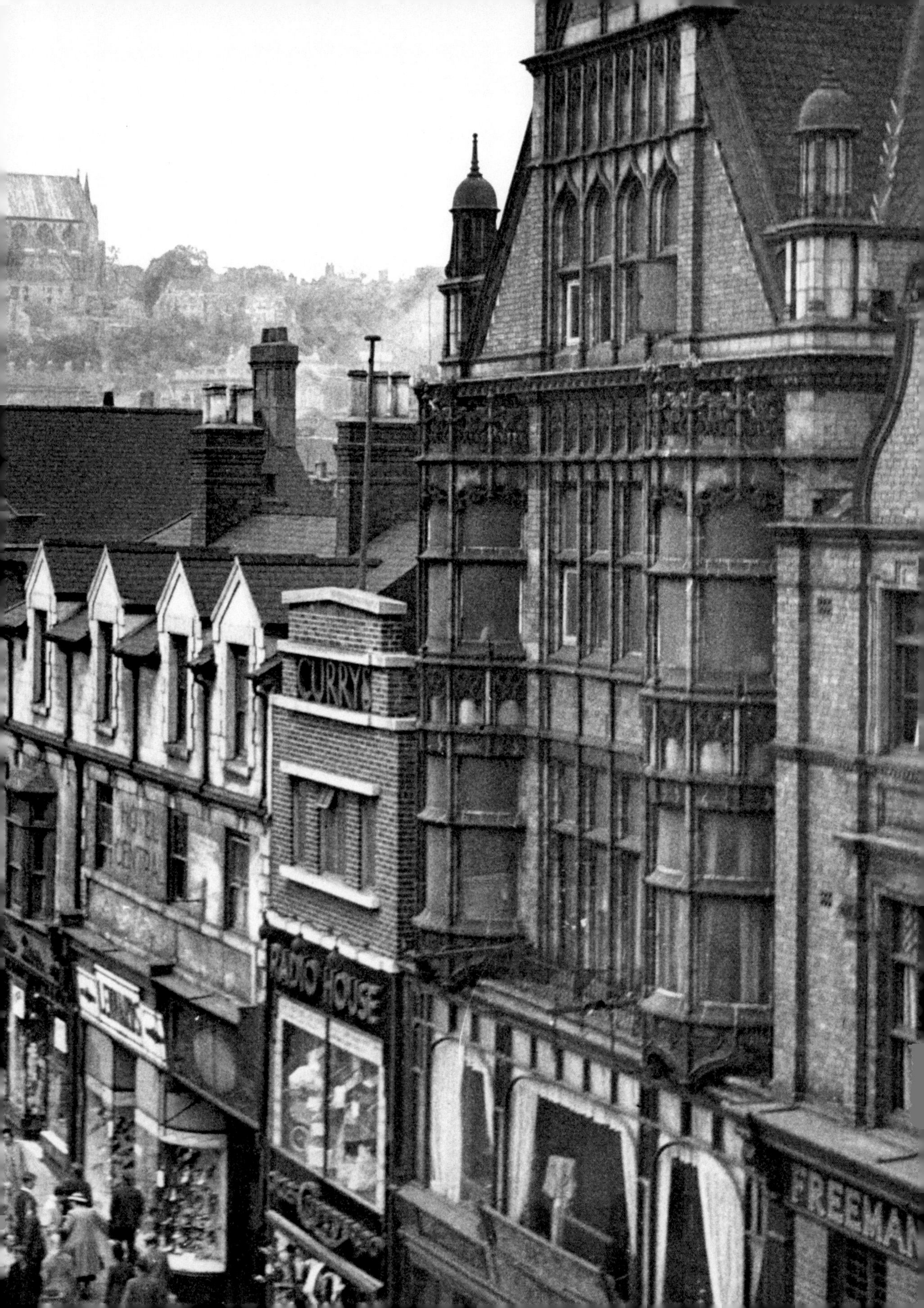
CURRYS
RADIO HOUSE
FREEMAN

A HISTORY & CELEBRATION

LINCOLN CITY FOOTBALL TEAM AT THE OLD JOHN O' GAUNT'S GROUND JUST OFF THE HIGH STREET IN 1895 ZZZ01591
(Lincolnshire County Council, Local Studies Collection)

There were various opportunities for leisure in Victorian Lincoln. In 1893 the Theatre Royal reopened the doors of its rebuilt premises, following a fire, with a performance of 'Charley's Aunt'. But there were also regular fairs and circus visits, first held in Orchard Street, later on the grounds of the cattle market in Monks Road, and later still moving to South Common. The biggest leisure event for the city as a whole occurred in August 1872 when the park known as the Arboretum opened on Monks Road. The park comprised ornamental planting, fountains, a bandstand and a statue of a large lion. The opening day festivities included five brass bands, a group of handbell ringers and 'Professor Banzo's Performing Dogs'. There was dancing and fireworks but if the promoters of the project had their way relatively little drinking; one of the objectives of the park was to tempt 'a man to enjoy himself with his wife and family in preference to accepting the pleasure of the public house.'

Organised football made its first appearance in the city in the 1860s. By 1883 an amateur team named Lincoln City had been formed. Three years later the team reached the last sixteen of the FA Cup competition, their march to the final cut short by Glasgow Rangers. Two years later they repeated the feat, this time losing out to Preston North End. The club did well in other competitions, however, and in 1891 took the momentous step of turning professional. In 1895 they moved to their new, and present, ground at Sincil Bank.

Many industrial towns and establishments produced football teams, their Saturday afternoon matches providing an ideal form of entertainment for the workforce. One such works team had its origins in the armaments factories in London, becoming known as the Woolwich Arsenal. They were Lincoln's opponents in their first league game of 1895, which they drew 1-1. The Victorian era came to an end for the club in 1902 with their most recent highest placing in the FA Cup, once again in the last sixteen but this time beaten by Derby County.

Victorian Lincoln

ALFRED, LORD TENNYSON

In 1809 Alfred Tennyson was born in the Lincolnshire village of Somersby. He quickly showed a talent for poetry and went to Trinity College, Cambridge in 1827. He published a number of collections, became one of the public's favourite poets and was made Poet Laureate in 1850. Among his most well known works are 'In Memoriam', 'The Lady of Shallot' and 'The Charge of the Light Brigade'. He died in 1892 and was buried in Westminster Abbey. However, the people of Lincoln wished to commemorate their links with a man thought by many to have been the world's greatest poet. In 1905 a statue was unveiled on Minster Green to the north of the cathedral. It shows Tennyson deep in thought, accompanied by his Siberian wolfhound, Karenina. The unveiling was conducted with much ceremony. There was a military band and the cathedral choir sang Tennyson's requiem poem, 'Crossing the Bar'. Today Lincoln's central library houses the Tennyson Research Centre.

'Half a league, half a league,
Half a league onward,
All in the valley of Death
Rode the six hundred.
"Forward, the Light Brigade!
"Charge for the guns!" he said:
Into the valley of Death
Rode the six hundred.'

The Charge of the Light Brigade, 1854

TENNYSON STATUE 1906 55109

A HISTORY & CELEBRATION

The government of Lincoln had for many years been idiosyncratic. The city council had managed to avoid levying a general rate on the inhabitants by making use of various other traditional forms of income such as rents, tolls and fines. By the later part of the 19th century this was no longer sustainable. There were issues of street paving and lighting, of waste disposal and sewerage, and the difficult problem of water supply. Fearing that they would be voted out of office, they doggedly resisted instituting a rate.

The Public Health Act of 1858 gave borough councils the power to deal in particular with the problem of sewage. Lincoln's councillors declined to implement the act until 1866 when, amid much acrimony, they took control of paving and street repairs, establishing a system of standardised rates. The sewage question was more difficult, yet the city's rivers were stagnant and polluted, so polluted they could not even be used for steam engine purposes let alone human uses! The Home Office sent an inspector in 1870 but it was not until 1876, and the threat by the Home Secretary of legal action, that steps were taken to resolve the problem.

During the 1880s and 1890s the city corporation became decidedly more active, undertaking various improvement works. A new road, Yarborough Road, was created to carry traffic around the western side of the city and private utility companies were bought up, including those supplying water and gas. In 1898 a new Corporation Electricity Works was established on Brayford Wharf North. Yet the output of the private generator station of Clayton and Shuttleworth was so much greater that in 1919 it was contracted to supply the demands of the city. In 1902 transport came under the eye of the corporation and they bought the Lincoln Tramways Company which ran from Bracebridge into the city.

Nevertheless one area not tackled effectively was that of the contaminated water supply. Consequently it was of little surprise to many when the city suffered a typhoid epidemic in 1904. Emergency measures were taken, including the delivery of clean water from Newark by special trains. Yet the outbreak continued for five months, struck down more than 1000 people and killed 127. Following this sorry episode a wholesome water supply was brought to the city from boreholes sunk at Elkesley in Nottinghamshire. The water eventually flowed into the city in 1911 and a massive water tower was constructed on Westgate just north of the castle to help regulate demand.

Lincoln then at the beginning of the 20th century was a thriving community that seemed to have left many of its troubles behind. The population labouring in the great industrial engineering works had employment, housing, entertainment and, at last, clean water. The streets were paved and lit at night and there were schools and hospitals. The world was, however, on the verge of great change and Lincoln, no longer a sleepy county town would have a vital part to play in it.

Victorian Lincoln

STEEP HILL 1906 55115

Little has changed in this part of the city since this photograph was taken nearly 100 years ago.

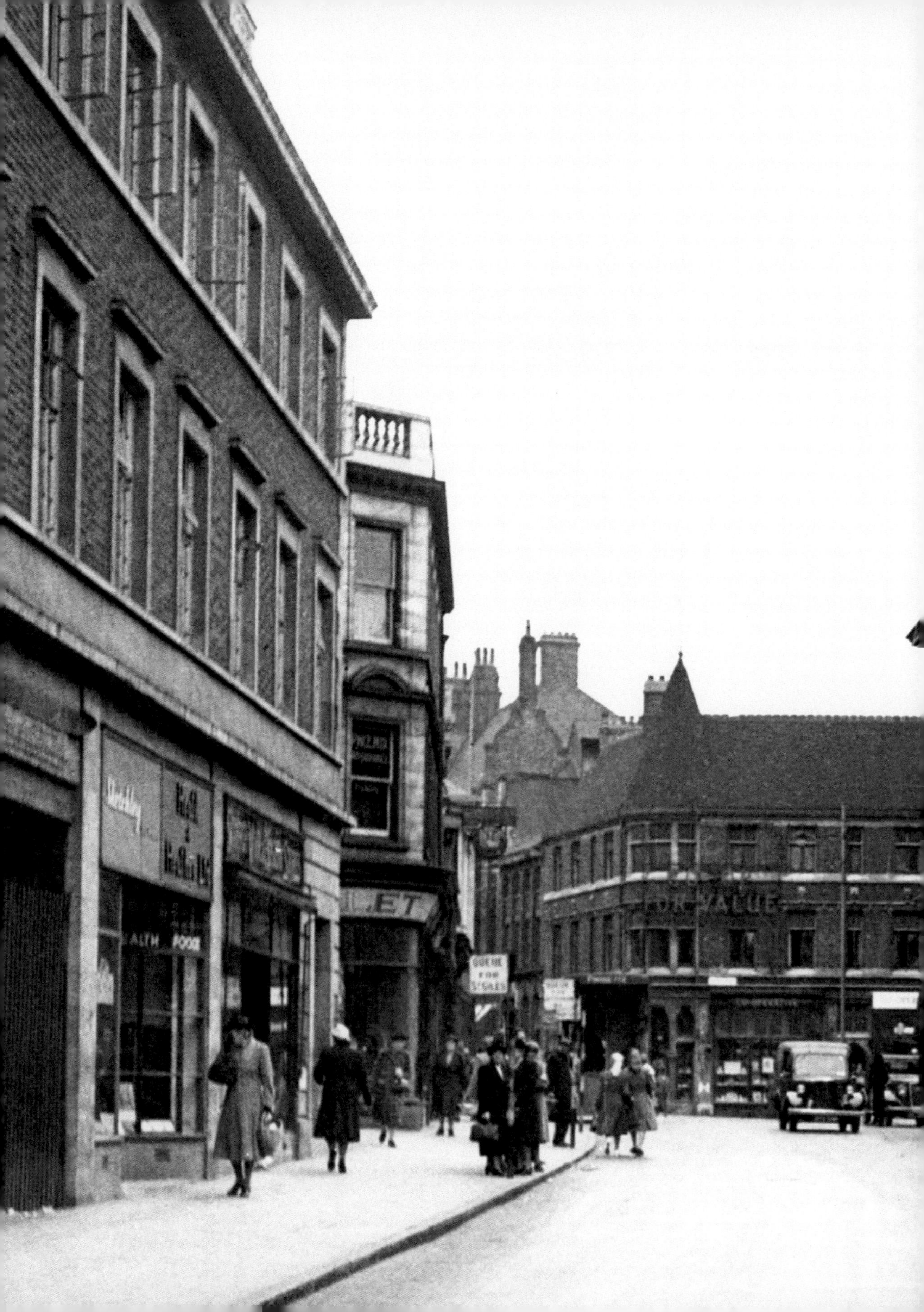
QUEUE FOR St GILES
FOR VALUE

CHAPTER FOUR
20TH CENTURY LINCOLN

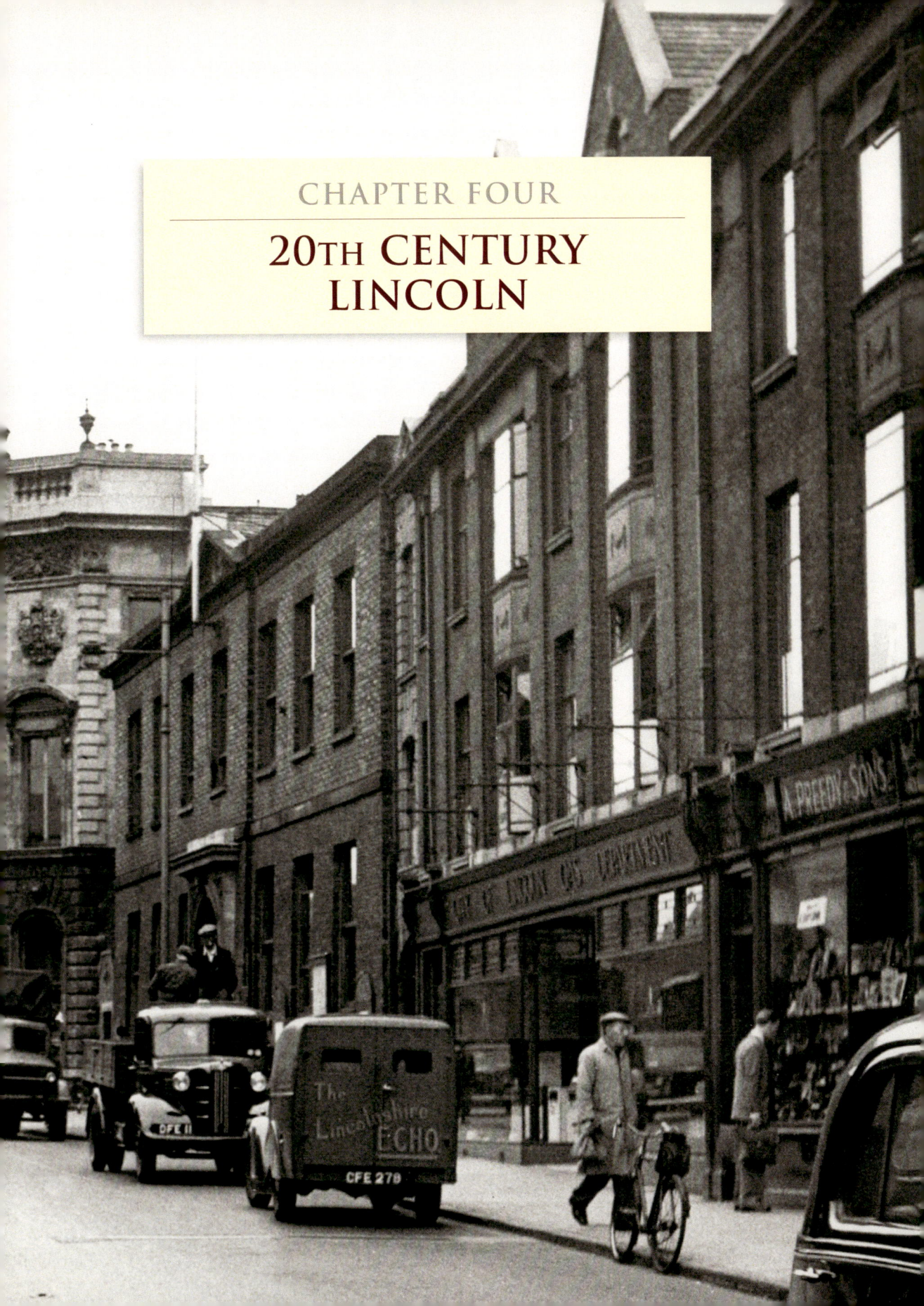

A HISTORY & CELEBRATION

EDWARDIAN VISITORS stepping off a train at one of the Lincoln railway stations and making their way up the High Street toward the Stonebow would have experienced the sights, sounds and smells of a thriving city. The streets were busy with people, market traders and richly decorated shops; there were few motorcars to endanger the pedestrian but a fair number of horses, carts, carriages and bicycles. Crossing the High Bridge and admiring the obelisk, surmounting a soon to be redundant water conduit, they might be tempted to check in at the long established and highly recommended Saracens Head Hotel. Lincoln, with its dynamic mix of county town atmosphere, industrial capacity and a body of fine aspiring citizens, was undoubtedly a model town of the era.

By 1922 Lincoln housed some 61,000 people, who were well served with a range of markets, shops, educational establishments and health care facilities. In 1878 the old County Hospital had been built in the city. This was gradually improved and modernised; in 1905 operating theatres were constructed and in 1912 a casualty ward opened. The new and present County Hospital opened in 1985.

For the population to expand further, without creating inner city slums, the city

The Saracens Head Hotel was one of Lincoln's finest during the 19th and 20th centuries. Ottakar's bookshop now occupies the northern half of the site, though the upper façade of the hotel remains. It is especially notable for the late Georgian ironwork of its balcony panels.

STONEBOW c1955 L49121

20th Century Lincoln

A HISTORY & CELEBRATION

ARMED MILITIA GUARDING LINCOLN CENTRAL STATION DURING THE NATIONAL RAILWAY STRIKE OF 1911
ZZZ01592 (Lincolnshire County Council, Local Studies Collection)

During 1911 there were various national and local industrial disputes over wages and conditions. In Lincoln armed militia were used to patrol the stations as workers joined the tumultuous national railway strike.

would need to be enlarged. The key to such enlargement was transport. In 1902 the corporation had taken possession of the company that ran horse-drawn trams from Bracebridge to the High Street. By 1905 the decision was made to electrify the route, using a system of studs concealed within the roadway. The mechanism was prone to faults, so in 1919 an improved overhead wire system was installed. The electric trams were finally superseded by motor buses in 1929.

But all was not well on the industrial relations front, especially in the sphere of transport. The political landscape was changing, with the rise of ever-stronger trade unions and the new Labour party with its socialist policies. Employers and government alike saw such change as threatening, even revolutionary, and steadfastly refused to accommodate the demands made for better working conditions and improvements in pay. In 1911 Lincoln's engineering unions called a strike. Though some unions settled quickly, the Boiler Makers Union refused to back down and the strike dragged on. In August a much more turbulent conflict broke out with the national rail strike. Although the strike had its origins elsewhere, it quickly spread to Lincoln and as many as 5,000 strikers from both industries came together for a mass protest near to St Mark's Station. By 11 o'clock in the evening the police had had enough. They confiscated banners and called on the strikers to disperse; when they did not they were baton charged by 80 constables. In the ensuing disorder that raged up and down the High Street dozens of shop windows were smashed. Eventually troops were called out. By the early hours of the morning calm returned, but dozens of people had been injured and two died.

But Edwardian Lincoln was not all about industrial muscle; the corporation had an

20TH CENTURY LINCOLN

interest in improving the minds of its citizens. Using powers provided by the 1892 Public Libraries Act, a City of Lincoln Public Library was established in 1894. It was first housed in the old Assembly Rooms over the Butter Market, but in 1914 a new library opened in Free School Lane. The building, designed by Sir Reginald Blomfield, was in part funded by the Carnegie foundation. Today it continues to serve as the county's Central Library. Immediately to the south of the library lay the old Greyfriars building where, in 1906, the corporation was persuaded to open a city museum. Nearly 100 years later, in 2004, the Greyfriars Museum finally closed its doors before moving to the new City and County Museum on Danesgate.

In September 1914 Britain was plunged into war, a war that would be different, a war that would be industrial. Ruston and Proctor used their experience of building farm machinery, which combined power units with wooden framing, to undertake aircraft production. By the middle of 1915 the company was turning out military aircraft. In all some 2,750 units were handed over to the Royal Flying Corp. Other manufacturers diverted resources into such work, making Lincoln one of the largest aircraft production sites in the world. Among the aircraft built were Sopwith Camels, Short

THE CENTRAL LIBRARY BUILT IN 1914 2004 L49709k (Craig Spence)

A HISTORY & CELEBRATION

THE GREYFRIARS BUILDING, ORIGINALLY THE INFIRMARY OF THE FRIARY DATING TO THE THIRTEENTH CENTURY 2004 L49710k (Craig Spence)

184 Seaplanes and Handley Page bombers. But other wartime necessities were also made, and made by women as well as men. Ruston's produced tens of thousands of engines, carriages, gun-fittings and even portable pigeon lofts. They also made half a million shells and bombs.

Lincoln is probably best known for the design, manufacture and production of one weapon in particular, the tank. In the summer of 1915 Lieutenant W G Wilson and the managing director of Wm Foster Ltd, William Tritton, combined to design an armoured war machine that would use caterpillar tracks. Within a few weeks the world's first prototype tank, 'Little Willie', was put through secret trials in Burton Park at the far end of Burton Road. Lessons were learnt and by January 1916 a new design was being tested. This was the 'mother' type. The government immediately ordered a hundred of these and they were manufactured during the summer of 1916, seeing their first action on 15 September at the battle of the Somme. William Tritton was knighted for his contribution and later the new road built through the area of the works was named after him. In 1983 one of these first tanks returned to

20th Century Lincoln

> ## Fact File
> ### Flight Testing
>
> *Many of the aircraft made in Lincoln during the First World War were delivered to the 'Number 4 Aircraft Acceptance Park', situated on West Common. There, Royal Flying Corp pilots tested each one – occasionally to destruction – before they were put into service.*

Lincoln. After restoration by Ruston's apprentices it was put on display at the Museum of Lincolnshire Life on Burton Road.

Peace finally came in 1918 and Lincoln attempted to return to normal. High on the list of priorities was a suitable war memorial to the city's fallen, yet money was scarce and despite several fund-raising initiatives it was 1922 before enough had been raised to construct a memorial. It was sited prominently at the east end of the church of St Benedict, facing the High Street.

THE WAR MEMORIAL AND ST BENEDICT'S CHURCH ON THE HIGH STREET 2004 L4971lk (Craig Spence)

MUMBY & SON Lᵀᴰ
NEWARK.
LEEDS.
LINCOLN.
WHOLESALE
CLOTHIERS

GIRLS WANTED

THE GLORY HOLE 1923   74639p

A HISTORY & CELEBRATION

THE TANK

WORKERS AT WM FOSTER LTD NEW WELLINGTON WORKS IN FRONT OF TANK c1916 ZZZ01593
(Lincolnshire County Council, Local Studies Collection)

Lincoln's greatest contribution to World War I was the invention and manufacture of the tank. First developed in 1915, the tank was put into full production the following year by Wm Foster Ltd at the New Wellington Works on New Boultham Road. Each tank was tested on mock trenches and obstacles, in an area to the south of the works just beyond the route of the high-level 'avoiding line' railway. Both company and workforce were very proud of their achievement and willingly posed for 'team' photographs such as the one shown here. A similar but separate photograph was posed with the factory's women war workers. The military value of the tank was quickly recognised and in 1917 General Sir Douglas Haig sent a formal telegram of congratulations to Foster's, where it was put it on display for all to see.

Copy of Telegram received from SIR DOUGLAS HAIG.

"The TANKS provided by your Department have rendered very valuable services in Battle near CAMBRAI. I beg you to accept and convey to all those under you whose skill and labour have produced the Tanks, the grateful thanks of the ARMY in FRANCE."

26.11.17.   D. HAIG.

COPY OF TELEGRAM FROM GENERAL DOUGLAS HAIG TO WM FOSTER LTD NOVEMBER 1917 ZZZ01594
(Lincolnshire County Council, Local Studies Collection)

20th Century Lincoln

The ending of military contracts caused many difficulties for Lincoln's manufacturers. In the case of Ruston and Proctor amalgamation was in the air. R Hornsby of Grantham, builders of oil engines, proposed the merger; Ruston and Hornsby Ltd was formed at the end of 1918. While the directors of the company may have been reassured, the business continued to struggle. By 1923 the joint Lincoln and Grantham workforce had fallen from 13,000 to 4,750. Many of the old product lines were resumed but in the new aircraft works the order books were empty. Instead Ruston and Hornsby entered the world of motor car production. They built very good cars, but they were if anything too good and too expensive. They did not sell well and in 1925 production ceased. Five years later a further amalgamation took place, Ruston and Hornsby had become an important builder of mechanical excavators so it was natural that a merger with Bucyrus-Erie, their equivalent in the United States of America, would be beneficial. Thus was born the new subsidiary company of Ruston-Bucyrus, which would become celebrated as the largest manufacturer of excavators in Europe.

Clayton and Shuttleworth did not do so well and had to shed several of their works. By 1924 the original Stamp End boiler works had been sold to Babcock and Wilcox who, among other things, produced mooring masts for the government's imperial airship service. Soon after, the famous R101 airship would be seen in the skies above Lincoln. Clayton and Shuttleworth laboured on until 1936. The closure of many of their works was devastating for the local community, as the 'Lincolnshire Chronicle' put it 'the disastrous end to so magnificent a business has had a tragic effect in the homes of the many former employees who are now workless.' Some elements of the company were viable, however, and Clayton Dewandre Co Ltd took over the Titanic Works until the late 1980s for motor engineering purposes.

It was against this background of economic depression that a number of town improvement schemes were undertaken. Two in particular were of great importance; first was the building of public housing by the city, the second was slum clearance. The Wragby Road housing scheme to the north-east of the city was first mooted in 1914 but the war had intervened, so it was not until 1920 that construction on the St Giles estate eventually commenced. Similar garden suburb schemes, but privately sponsored, were embarked upon at Boultham and Swanpool. Slum clearance programmes were instituted at the beginning of the 1930s; many of these areas of housing lay in the centre of the city and were also associated with road-widening activities.

Within the town centre several drastic changes to the built environment went ahead, not with the approval of all the city's inhabitants. In the 1920s the diocesan authorities decided to dispose of two city churches: St Benedict on the High Street and St Peter-at-Arches just north of the Stonebow. Lincoln's antiquarian and historical societies fought vigorous campaigns to save both buildings, in the case of St Benedict they

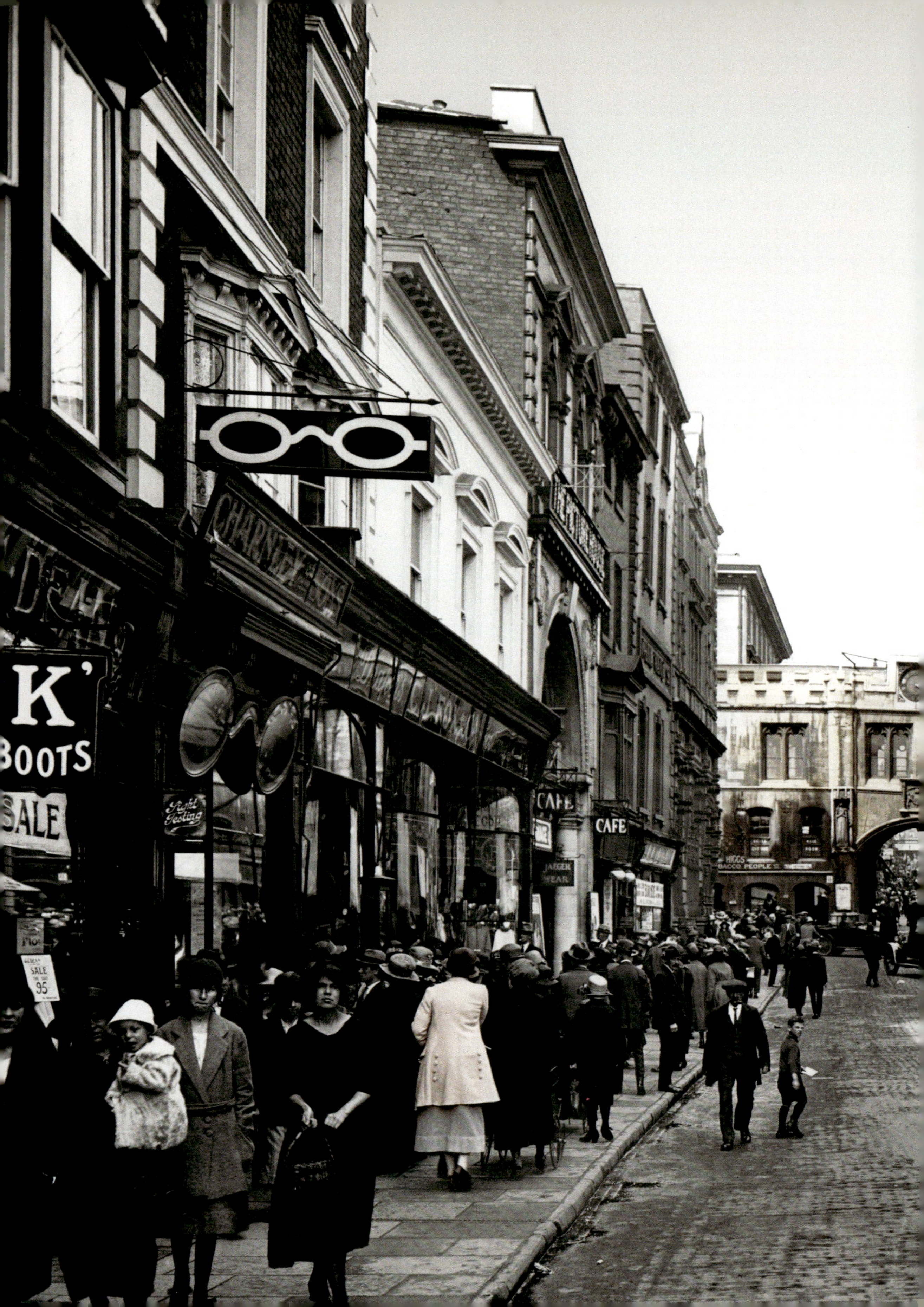
K'
BOOTS
SALE
Sight Testing
CAFE
CAFE
JAEGER WEAR

STONEBOW 1923 74634p

A HISTORY & CELEBRATION

POTTER GATE AND CATHEDRAL c1950 L49054

In 1938 Potter Gate, part of the cathedral close wall since the 14th century, was left isolated on a traffic island by the construction of the roadway on its eastern side.

were mostly successful, they had less success with St Peter. The church was demolished in 1933 as part of a road-widening scheme for Silver Street. Nevertheless the authorities agreed that the church could be dismantled, rather than destroyed. It was rebuilt as the parish church of St Giles on the new housing estate. Elements of the façade of the Butter Market, demolished in 1937, were also kept and mounted on the northern side of the new Central Market built on Sincil Street in 1938.

Other changes recognised the value of the historic buildings of the city. In Uphill there were works of restoration around Castle Hill and at the cathedral. In Castle Hill a number of houses that crowded the east gate of the

20TH CENTURY LINCOLN

castle were removed in the 1930s, revealing a clearer view of the castle walls. On the north side of the square adjacent to Bailgate, the impressive 16th century half-timbered building was restored in 1929 at the expense of the National Provincial Bank. It now houses one of the city's tourist information offices.

Restoration work on the cathedral was much more dramatic and much more necessary. In 1921 it was realised that the towers of the cathedral were in danger of collapse and that extensive works would have to be undertaken to protect them.

For 11 years the building was covered in enormous timber scaffolds both inside and out, while teams of masons conducted their work. They used innovative stone conservation techniques, employing Robey's compressors to power both drills and high-pressure water sprays.

ST PETER-AT-ARCHES CHURCH BEING DISMANTLED c1932 ZZZ01595 (Lincolnshire County Council, Local Studies Collection)

In the background can be seen the old Butter Market of 1736.

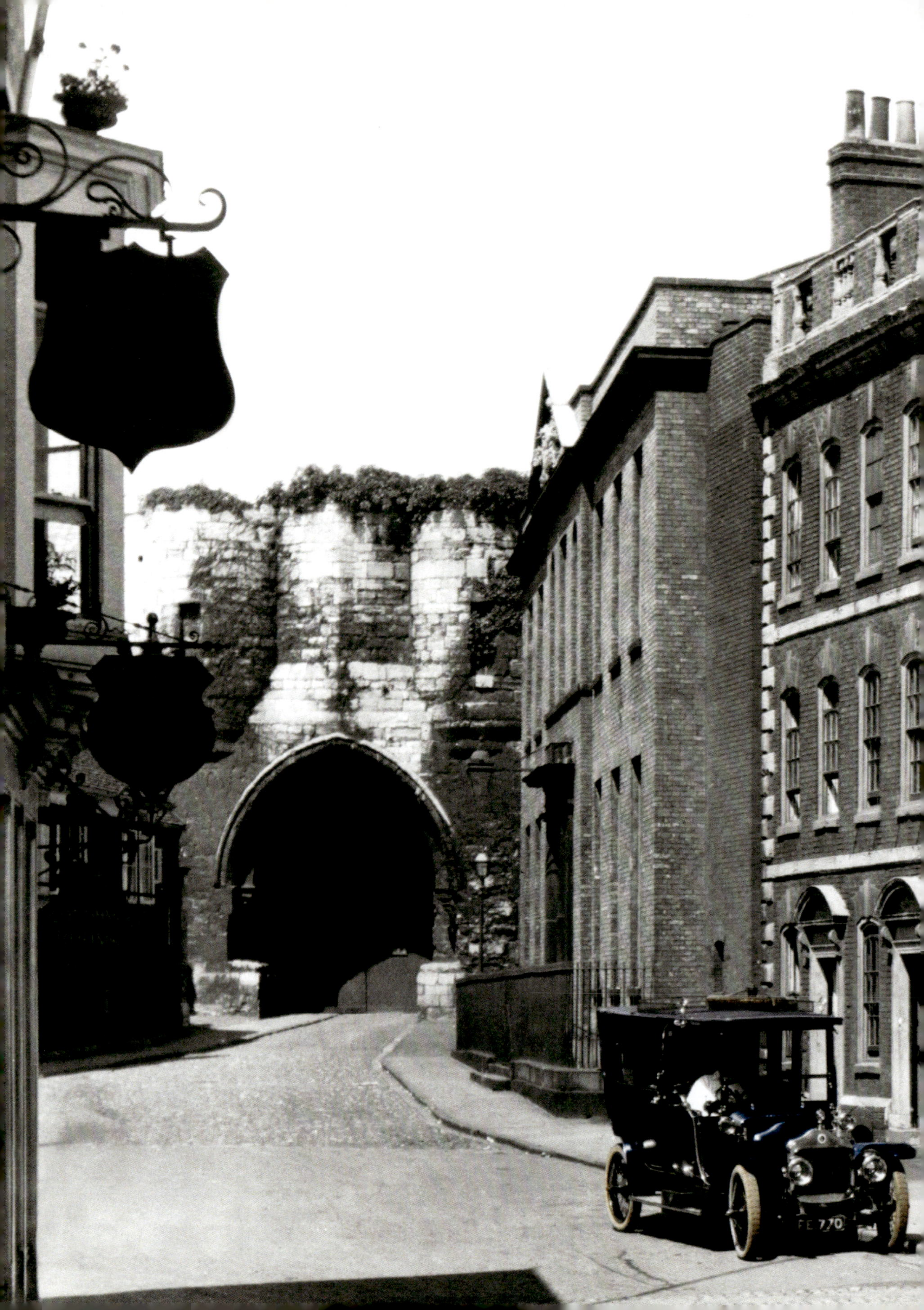
FE 770

CASTLE HILL 1906 55115ap

A HISTORY & CELEBRATION

HIGH BRIDGE AND THE OBELISK

HIGH BRIDGE 1923 74637

High Bridge originally housed a chapel dedicated to St Thomas. This was eventually removed and in its place an obelisk was erected in 1762. The obelisk became a well-known feature of Lincoln High Street for the next two centuries. The base of the structure also served to house one of the city's water conduits, but the conduits were made redundant when the new supply was turned on in 1911. Fearing that the weight of the monument was damaging the bridge, it was removed in February 1939. Many thought it lost for ever but some 40 years later it was to reappear in the centre of the new St Marks Retail Park, built after the railway station of that name had been demolished in the 1980s.

THE OBELISK IN ST MARKS RETAIL PARK 2004 L49712k (Craig Spence)

20th Century Lincoln

A further enhancement to the city during the 1920s was the construction of the Usher Art Gallery; named after its founder James Ward Usher, a highly successful watch and clock dealer who had premises at 192 High Street. James Usher built up a considerable collection of antique watches, porcelain and miniatures, which he donated to the new gallery. The Prince of Wales, later Edward VIII, opened the building in 1927.

Another form of visual entertainment enjoyed by many throughout the 20th century was the cinema. Lincoln's first film showings took place in St Hugh's church hall on Monks Road in 1909. Similar early screenings occurred at the Theatre Royal and in the new Corn Exchange. During the following decades a number of purpose-built cinemas were constructed such the Grand and the Lincoln Picture House, later renamed the Regal, both on the High Street. In the 1930s larger auditoria were needed and the Savoy, later known as the ABC, and the Ritz were built. The ABC closed its doors in 1986, the Ritz, on the lower High Street, in 1997.

The people of Lincoln have always enjoyed their sport, and central to this have been the fortunes of the racetrack to the west

THE ART GALLERY c1950 L49005

A HISTORY & CELEBRATION

> ### Fact File
>
> ### 'The Wild and the Willing'
>
> *The producers of the 1962 film 'The Wild and the Willing' chose Lincoln as the ideal location for their story of the delinquent life of a group of university students, this despite the fact that Lincoln had never had a university. The film was notable for providing debuts for John Hurt, Ian McShane and Samantha Eggar. It also featured Johnny Briggs, better known as Mike Baldwin of 'Coronation Street'.*

HIGH STREET c1950 L49028p

of the city and Lincoln City Football Club, nicknamed the Imps. The first real success of the 20th century for the Imps came in 1932 with the third division championship. The heady heights of the second division did not last long, however, and the following season saw relegation. In 1948, after a break during the Second World War, they again achieved promotion but unbelievably again suffered immediate relegation. In 1952, however, the Imps made it to the second division where they stayed until 1961. Having been under the stewardship of Bill Anderson since the war the club had eventually to turn to other managers. In the 1970s a former player, Graham Taylor, was appointed. The following six years were some of the best in the club's history. After that came disaster, first real and then footballing. During the last game of the 1985 season away at Bradford City, the grandstand caught fire. Two Lincoln fans died in the inferno, they are commemorated in the name of a new stand opened at Sincil Bank in 1990 - the Stacey West Stand. The footballing disaster occurred in 1987 when the club

20TH CENTURY LINCOLN

were relegated out of the Football League, yet in true Imps style the next season saw instant promotion. The most recent drama for the club came in 2003 with their participation in the division three play-off final against Bournemouth, a game they unfortunately lost 5-2. Unperturbed, Lincoln welcomed the team home with a street parade and civic reception.

Returning to the late 1930s, we find Lincoln once again turning the attention

A HISTORY & CELEBRATION

RACING IN LINCOLN

Horse racing in Lincoln is first recorded in the 16th century, and King James I was certainly entertained by racing on Lincoln Heath during his visit in 1617. Annual racing events began in 1680 and continued on the Heath until 1773, after which they were relocated to the West Common. In time the races became a regular three-day meeting held each spring. The most celebrated race was the Lincolnshire Handicap, first run in 1849. Racing continued until the 1960s, when falling attendance and the ending of financial support from the Racing Levy Board signalled the end. Despite lobbying by the city council it was decided in 1964 that the races would have to stop. The famous 'Lincoln Handicap', as it is now known, was transferred to Doncaster. Here it remains central to the flat-racing calendar, being the opening race of the season. Beside Saxilby Road the old grandstand still looks down on West Common, a forlorn reminder of Lincoln's racing past.

of its manufacturing resources toward impending war. One of the most surprising projects was the creation of a gigantic trench-digging machine by Ruston-Bucyrus. Known as 'Nellie', it was a pet project of Winston Churchill; by the time war came the concept was, however, redundant. Of more use were the tens of thousands of diesel engines turned out by the Lincoln works, also numerous armoured vehicles including Matilda tanks. During the war Lincolnshire was home to dozens of RAF bases, including many of Bomber Command. Lincoln itself saw an ever-increasing number of service personnel passing through or taking leave in the city. Among several airfields situated close by were RAF Waddington, Scampton and Skellingthorpe; the first two remain operational today.

Despite a number of post-war setbacks, particularly in the engineering sector, Lincoln continued to grow. By 1971 the population of the city had increased only marginally above the earlier 20th century figures to reach